Making Sense of the Econ...

Making Sense of the Economy

Roger Martin-Fagg
Programme Director
Company Programmes
Henley Management College

Australia • Canada • Mexico • Singapore • Spain • United Kingdom • United States

Making Sense of the Economy

Copyright ©1996 Roger Martin-Fagg

The Thomson Learning logo is a registered
trademark used herein under licence

British Library Cataloguing-in-Publication Data
A catalogue record for this book is available from the British Library

First Edition 1996
Reprinted 1999
Reprinted 2000 by Thomson Learning

Typeset in the UK by J&L Composition Ltd, Filey, North Yorkshire
Printed in the UK by TJ International Ltd, Padstow, Cornwall

ISBN 1-86152-521-4

Thomson Learning
Berkshire House
168–173 High Holborn
London WC1V 7AA
UK

http://www.thomsonlearning.co.uk

To Penny and Katie

Contents

List of figures and tables   viii ix
Acknowledgements   x
Series editor's preface   xi
Introduction   1

1 Economics and economists   4
2 Measuring the Gross Domestic Product   12
3 What causes changes in the level of GDP?   21
4 Economic policy and a dynamic system:
    the business cycle   36
5 Money and how it is manufactured   63
6 The government and the money supply   71
7 Linkages between the components of the system   94
8 The balance of payments and trade   105
9 International linkages: the exchange rate and
    international money flows   125
10 Forecasting the economy   149

Conclusion and self-assessment test   167
Appendix A: Equilibrium: the difference between
planned and actual   174
Appendix B: Is the economy a mechanical system
or an organic system   177
Appendix C: The problem of savings and investment
behaviour   183
Appendix D: The Monetarist School and others   187
Appendix E: Stocks and flows   191
Appendix F: Glossary of terms   194

Figures and tables

FIGURES

3.1   A balanced growth economy   33
3.2   An unbalanced growth economy   33
3.3   Slumpflation   34
3.4   Stagflation   34
4.1   Sales forecast   42
4.2   UK GDP growth and change in stocks   45
4.3   Expenditure on durables and non-durables 1949–95   49
4.4   The stages of the cycle   52
4.5   Cyclical nature of the USA   55
4.6   Cyclical nature of Japan   55
4.7   Cyclical nature of Germany   56
4.8   Productive potential   58
4.9   The economic picture   59
4.10 The relationship between relative international
      domestic demand and the balance of payments   61
4.11 The UK output gap   61
5.1   Summary of Lloyds Bank's balance sheets   69
7.1   Behaviour of the financial markets   101
7.2   Inflation adjusted M4, GDP and retail sales   103
8.1   World trade   113
8.2   The 'J' curve   118
8.3   The global system of payments   120
9.1   The behaviour of the real exchange rate   145
9.2   The effect of an overvalued currency   147
9.3   The effect of an undervalued currency   148

10.1	Summary of the Lombard Street Ltd forecasting approach	155
10.2	The Keynesian forecasting approach	156
10.3	The stages of the cycle	158
10.4	Schematic representation of the business cycle	161
10.5	The cyclical indicators	164
B.1	(Appendix B) The global system of payments	181

TABLES

8.1	UK balance of payments 1989	106
8.2	Companies deriving at least 20% of trading profits from the EC	115
9.1	Foreign exchange market turnover and foreign trade	131
9.2	EMS European currency unit rates	136
9.3	The impact of the exchange rate	138
10.1	The cyclical indicators	163

Acknowledgements

Over the years, numerous people at both Thames Valley University and Henley Management College have, as participants in my sessions, influencd my approach to the subject. I am grateful to all those who kept asking why and pushed for straight, clear answers. This book is the result of their quest for understanding.

I am grateful to Christa Bond and Trisha Hyde for their word processing skills and their patience; there were many redrafts, what follows is the end result. Any errors or omissions of course are mine.

Series editor's preface

Successful managers of the 90s know it is no longer enough to be competent at core management skills. Those who are developing themselves for the next century realize that a knowledge of the broader environment in which they operate is essential.

A key part of our strategic review is to be able to understand changes taking place in the economic environment. This is important for those employed by organizations and even more important for the growing number of people who are self-employed. With an understanding of how to interpret the economic environment, managers are able to make more informed, realistic business forecasts.

Making Sense of the Economy has been written for those managers who want to take their first steps in understanding economies. It gives a good basic introduction to the subject and will enable managers to understand the market economy, government economic policy, the concept of money, the role of commercial banks and the operation of the central bank. Managers, as an added benefit, may even be able to manage their own finances more effectively as a result of reading this book.

Making Sense of the Economy is also suitable for managers needing to operate internationally. Chapters are included on balance of payments and trade flows and how the currency market works.

The Self-Development concept of the book is handled slightly differently. Each chapter concludes with a summary to give managers a better chance of understanding the key concepts introduced in that chapter. At the end of the book managers are encouraged to complete a self-assessment test, with answers, to check understanding.

Roger Martin-Fagg is a Client Director and member of the teaching faculty at Henley Management College. He is also known for his consulting and teaching and particularly for his skills of communicating an understanding of the economic environment and business strategy in a lively and interesting way. I have encouraged Roger to transfer these skills to write a book to complement his face-to-face teaching.

The Self-Development Series For Managers, which includes Making Sense of the Economy, is now well established. The series is designed to develop core skills and understanding needed by managers to be successful. Making Sense of the Economy complements step-by-step competitive strategy. Coverage is also given to developing core personal skills and functional skills, including marketing and accounting for managers.

Jane Cranwell-Ward
Series Editor

Introduction

I have written this book for anyone who feels the need to know more about how an economy works but who feels uncomfortable with indigestible theory explained using algebra.

I have assumed that you the reader will not be trying to pass an examination in economics, but you will be trying to find out how the business world works and about the links between markets. You may be at stage one of an MBA programme, you may be doing a business studies diploma or degree; if so this book will help you get to grips with some of the basics.

You may be someone who wants to improve their understanding of the world we live in and in particular wish to manage your financial affairs with greater background knowledge.

You may just want to be able to read the financial pages of the quality newspapers and place them in context.

I have tried to simplify wherever possible, I have tried to avoid jargon and at times give practical examples.

The book is organized in a traditional way.

At the end of each chapter you will find a short summary of the main points covered. At the end of the book there are a number of appendices which go deeper into some of the issues raised in the main body of the book.

Ideally you should try and read the whole book from start to finish to get a broad overview of the subject, skipping the bits you find difficult. Then re-read to obtain a deeper understanding.

Each chapter flows on from the preceding one in a sequence which is designed to build and broaden your understanding. Where relevant, evidence is presented in the form of charts or tables.

THE STRUCTURE OF THE BOOK

Chapter 1 defines the subject, places it in historical context and discusses the basic characteristics of a market economy.

Chapter 2 looks at the way in which the output of an economy is measured and some of the problems with the measurement; there is a detailed break down of the output of the UK economy presented in such a way that you can see how the individual elements of the economy fit together. The chapter goes on to develop the basic model of a market economy and explains some fundamental characteristics and relationships. It introduces the concept of the multiplier and the balance between big flows through the system. It shows the consequences of imbalance in the systems – leading to either inflation, deflation or stagflation (all of which are explained).

Chapter 3 introduces Government objectives and economic policy. It shows the links and what are called lagged effects between changes in policy and the time it takes for people to respond. It explains clearly what causes recessions by linking policy changes with the decisions businessmen take. It illustrates the concept of the multiplier and its interaction with the investment accelerator, using both as explanations for the business cycle. The stages of the business cycle are explained with reference to the UK. The USA, Japanese and German cycles are also illustrated.

At this stage in the book, the reader should have a good overview of the characteristics of a market economy, in particular the sources of instability.

Chapter 4 makes a step change in economic thinking and analysis in introducing the concept of money and the role of commercial banks as manufacturers of money. This is a complex area, so I have deliberately placed the analysis in three chapters; Chapter four shows how commercial banks create money. **Chapter 5** puts monetary creation in the context of Government Policy and the operation of the Central Bank. It also has a section on personal finance to show how you can play an active role in the monetary system and make a return.

Chapter 6 pulls the strands together and shows the linkages between individual investment decisions and the overall level of economic activity. It explains the rationale for purchasing shares, shows how shares relative to other forms of personal investment (such as bonds or cash) perform through the business cycle. It doesn't show you how to get rich quick, but it will enable you to make better personal finance decisions.

By this stage in the book, many readers will be wondering how international events have an impact on a domestic system and the basis for trade. So **Chapter 7** discusses the structure and nature of the balance of payments and trade flows; it explains why there is so much misunderstanding of the balance of payments.

Chapter 8 is essential reading for anyone who needs foreign currency. It explains how the currency market works. It shows the effect of currency movements on export prices and discusses the impact of this on profit margins. It explains how the Exchange Rate Mechanism works, and shows what section of the Financial Times to read for further information.

Having got this far in the book, the average reader will now want to use their new knowledge to turn data on the economy into information to enable them to make better forecasts of either their business revenues and profits or on the return of their personal investments.

Chapter 9 is all about forecasting the economy without the need for massive computing power. It highlights the key indicators of activity, shows how they behave and where they can be found. It is essential reading for anyone who has to take a view on the future, before putting together a business plan or personal financial plan.

At the end of the book is a self-assessment test, with the answers. Use the test to check your understanding. Re-read the parts you get wrong. I hope you enjoy reading the book.

1 *Economics and economists*

Man has been around a lot longer than the subject 'Economics'. And man has spent most of his time when not asleep trying to improve his material well-being. The history of mankind is one of continuous improvements in living conditions, through increased individual effort.

For centuries, material expansion proceeded at a very slow pace, limited by the weather and the productivity of the land. It is estimated that between AD500 and AD1500, the material output of Europe only grew by 0.5% per year. (Today we are used to at least 2.5% per year).

The rate of growth began to accelerate around 1500 and by 1700 it is estimated that material output had doubled. This dramatic change got people thinking. By 1700, an individual would in his life-time notice the changes taking place around him. The pace of expansion and change was unprecedented in man's existence; it attracted the attention of individuals such as Thomas Malhus, Adam Smith, David Ricardo and Karl Marx. They were concerned to discover and explain why material well-being was increasing, and the circumstances under which it might continue. Thus a subject was born as scholars of philosophy, politics and history tried to understand the world around them.

A Scottish academic, Adam Smith, published in 1776 the *Wealth of Nations*. It attempted to explain how economies worked and why some countries were so much richer than others. Smith was a keen observer of his world which was changing rapidly as Great Britain experienced the Industrial Revolution. His book contains a model of how the economy is thought to operate, (a theory) with supporting evidence.

4

Smith can be labelled the first great economist; he first of all observed man's behaviour and its outcomes and then tried to explain it all. Thus the subject came into existence as a great mix of sociology, politics and philosophy. Since then, regrettably, the subject has been refined, sub-divided, and in our universities become increasingly rarified and precise, and thus of little benefit to those who seek explanations of the way things are and how it all works.

The result of academic refinement is a subject split into two main areas. (Something Adam Smith could not have agreed with). Micro economics is essentially the theory of what determines the individual price of something, for example a Mars Bar.

Micro economic theory would (its supporters claim) be able to explain:

1 how the price of a Mars Bar is determined
2 how many Mars Bars will be produced per period
3 how the wage rates for production line operatives are determined.

Macro economic theory attempts to explain the average level of all prices in an economy and changes in that level; it attempts to explain the total output produced by a country and changes in the level of that output. It also attempts to explain the levels of employment and unemployment.

So in essence, micro economics tries to explain the behaviour of individual components of the system, and macro economics tries to explain the workings of the system as a whole.

Adam Smith didn't make any distinction between micro and macro. For him, the economy was a total system which operated within the context of society – he saw enlightened self-interest as the driving force of a successful economy. He defined living standards in terms of material and moral standards and fully recognized that each individual was part of society as a whole which set the moral conditions under which individuals operated.

Britain was at its peak of world power and influence around 1870; the Victorian era was characterized by certainty in life; everyone knew their place in society. At this time, the physical sciences made enormous strides in their development. The application of mathematics as a means of rational analysis was widespread, and scientists saw the physical world as a complex machine which could be explained.

At Manchester University William Jevons, a physicist, introduced mathematical analysis to economics and with it introduced certainty to the subject. The main issue was a micro economic one; how could scarce resources be allocated in the most efficient manner? Growth was taken for granted; economic fluctuations ignored. The subject developed into a theory of general equilibrium, which essentially meant the relationships between inputs and outputs were fixed and predetermined, with markets operated by rational men. This view of the world prevailed until the late 1920s when it was quite clear that it could not explain the then high levels of unemployment and was comprehensively challenged by Maynard Keynes, who showed that the behaviour of the economy as a whole was different from the behaviour of its component parts, and who recognized that as societies develop so people's behaviour changes; and the relationships between input and output become imprecise.

Keynes was able to show that full employment of resources was not a natural state of affairs; indeed he argued that an economy needed to be actively managed to achieve full employment.

Keynesian demand management policies were applied throughout the fifties and sixties in most countries of the world. It was a period of unprecedented growth and prosperity.

Things began to go wrong after 1973 as most countries experienced lower rates of growth and higher average levels of inflation.

By 1980, Keynesian principles were being replaced by those of an earlier time (pre-1920) as countries desperately tried to solve their lower growth and high inflation problems.

At present economics and economists are in disarray. The world has developed faster than the subject. The Victorians saw the economy as a huge mechanical system driven by rational behaviour. Keynes showed how important emotions were in the system, and importance of feel good or feel bad as drivers of behaviour. The present sees the subject torn apart by the various schools of thought. On the one side are those who believe the economy will always tend towards full employment, providing Government doesn't get in the way; on the other side there are those who believe Government must actively promote full employment. Then there are those who are developing chaos theory to show

how economies go through periodic 'explosions' before beginning to settle down to a period of comparative stability.

Most of these areas are beyond the scope of this book. But it is important that you, the reader, realize that the subject is being continuously developed and refined. So if an economist with great authority states A or B or C, he or she is either suffering from myopia, or arrogance based on ignorance.

Economics as a subject cannot fully explain why so many things are as they are. But as this book tries to, it can increase our understanding of an extremely complex system devised and run by man.

HOW TO SHARE OUT SOMETHING IN SHORT SUPPLY?

Man has in his existence, devised only two methods of sharing things in short supply. The first involves pricing; the second involves sharing, on a first come first served basis.

A market economy uses price to allocate goods in short supply. Adam Smith in the *Wealth of Nations* described at length how goods were allocated in the UK economy in the 1760s, he called it *the invisible hand*.

The invisible hand works on the basis of transactions between willing buyers and willing sellers. The seller will decide how many, say, shoes can be sold at a predetermined price, size, colour and style. He will work out the costs involved in making them, calculate how much profit he will make on each pair, and then decide whether or not to make them.

The buyer will decide whether the shoes offered at a predetermined price represent good value for money (compared to all the other things, including shoes, which are offered for sale). If the buyer decides to purchase, the shoes are exchanged for money. Because shoe manufacturers try to meet buyer requirements there will be a wide range of prices, styles and colours offered in the market. This system produces shoes which range in price from £8 to £600. If the buyers reject the £600 pair of shoes, they will remain unsold, and the seller will not make any more; but if the buyers want more £8 shoes than are available, two things will happen: first, the price will rise and second, more shoes will be produced.

Thus the invisible hand is ensuring buyers and sellers exchange goods for money to mutual benefit. The role of profit is important: the seller will only make shoes if they believe the profit is significant to compensate them for time, effort and risk. The market system now operates in almost all countries of the world. It is not necessarily fair, but it does seem to achieve a great improvement in man's living conditions than the alternative which has been rejected after sixty years of failure.

The alternative is the *command system.*

The command system works as follows. A central committee decides what the population should have, and then instructs state owned factories and co-operatives to make these things. The consumer has no direct say in quality, colour or design, i.e. no real choice. The Soviet style command economy has only enjoyed a short existence, 1922–89. It failed because it didn't meet the wants and needs of people; it produced too much of some things and not enough of others and at a level of quality lower than that produced by a market economy.

WHAT IS WEALTH AND PROSPERITY?

We assess wealth and measure prosperity by measuring the value of things people own.

A Dinka tribesman in Southern Sudan would assess his wealth according to the number of cattle he owned (rather than their market price).

Economists have always wrestled with the measurement of wealth and most are unhappy with the way it is done but cannot think of a better way.

A country's wealth is measured by estimating the value of all its assets. Something which is difficult to do; for example, North Sea Oil is part of our wealth – how do we assess its value? The approach is to take the current price per barrel and multiply it by the estimated reserves in barrels.

Wealth and income are different. Wealth is the value of things you possess; income is something you receive. Wealth is a stock, whereas income is a flow. Wealthy people often have a small income and young, high income earners are often not very wealthy, because they have limited assets.

The size of a country's economy is estimated not from its wealth, but from its current income. Before the estimates can be prepared, economists and statisticians have to decide what should and should not be included, and then find a way of measuring it.

Comprehensive estimates of the size of the UK economy were not available until the end of the 1930s. A number of conventions were established then which still apply today.

The first convention is that the estimates are based on monetary transactions, which are usually the result of people buying and selling things for money. Thus any activity which doesn't involve a monetary transaction doesn't get measured.

In New Zealand there is a tradition of people giving each other a day's labour at the weekend in order to dig gardens, paint houses and their tin roofs. Because there is no monetary exchange this activity is not measured. If each New Zealander paid the other for a day's work, then it would be measured. In this way the work of a housewife cleaning, cooking and rearing children is not measured, but the work of a paid nanny is.

Many African States have small economies as estimated according to the convention. This is because the bulk of activity takes place on a barter or not for money basis. Subsistence agriculture is of zero value according to the conventional measures. So if some African subsistence farmers sold goods to each other instead of exchanging them, the size of the economy would increase according to the statistics and yet there is physically no increase in the amount of things available to the population.

The conventional approach underestimates the size of all economies. It doesn't measure wealth either. So what does is measure?

The conventional approach measures the added value produced by man's activity.

Assume you purchase a chest of tea for £10. It contains 100lbs of tea. You bag the tea up into 1lb bags, place a label on each, and sell them for 50 pence each.

The added value is selling price less cost of purchased inputs.

i.e. 50p per lb bags. 10p per lb equals 40p per lb.
or 40p × 100 = £40

The official definition of added value is:

sales value less cost of materials and other purchased goods and services.

Therefore added value = wages plus profit.

The Gross Domestic Product is the sum of the estimated added value produced by activity in an economy.

The estimates do not measure the value of all transactions, only those transactions which add value.

Back to the tea example, the total value of all transactions is £60, made up of the tea chest at £10, plus 100 one pound bags sold at 50 pence = £50.

But the added value is £40.

Added value is always wages and profit in some combination. It's what is left of revenue after materials and other purchases of goods and services have been deducted.

So the added value is £40.

Thus there is a difference between the total value of transactions and the value of economic activity. The value of transactions is many times larger than the value of economic activity.

For the UK, the value of economic activity in 1995 is estimated at £700 Bn (where 1Bn is a thousand million) but the value of transactions (estimated from cheques cleared by value) is 42 times larger.

So how is the value of economic activity determined?

A system of National Accounts estimates the sum of the value of goods and services produced in the economy during a particular period, usually one year.

The accounting system was first used in the mid-1930s and has been adapted but not fundamentally changed since.

The basic structure is repeated in Chapter 2 and is based on an inescapable logic, which is that economic activity can be estimated from

1   the final expenditure of the system
2   the sum of wages and profit in the system
3   the sum of value of final output.

But we have already said that the total value of transactions will be many times the value of economic activity. This is because of double counting, and the sale of existing assets by one person to another.

The sum of the value added over all stages of production, distribution and retail must be equal to the value of the final product (excluding VAT).

The value added of a firm which is not paid to other producers must be wages, salaries and profits, which together must be the sum of incomes.

In the next chapter the National Accounts for the UK are described.

2 Measuring the gross domestic product of the UK

THE GROSS DOMESTIC PRODUCT (GDP) OF THE UNITED KINGDOM

The Gross Domestic Product is an estimate of the final value of goods and services sold in the economy at a given point in time, measured at market prices, and with the value of imports subtracted. The figures are necessarily estimates and subject to revisions years later.

The table below shows the estimates for the GDP of the United Kingdom at market prices. It was measured by adding up all expenditure in the economy:

A Consumers' expenditure excludes expenditure on new houses (see D). Welfare payments are included.

B This item is the amount Central Government spends on consumption of materials, fuels, food, etc. It does not include welfare payments.

C This item is the same as B but at the local level.

D This item includes expenditure on new houses, plant and equipment, schools, hospitals, motorways and setting-up telecommunication networks.

E This figure is a stock adjustment figure. In a period of destocking this will be negative. It shows the movement in stocks.

F This figure includes spending on imports but excludes the value of exports.

G Here the value of exports of goods and services is added in.

H Total final expenditure inclusive of tax, subsidies, etc.

	£billion 1987	£billion 1991	£billion 1993	Refer to:
Consumers' expenditure	267.5	367.8	405.6	A
plus Central Government final consumption	52.0	74.4	88.2	B
plus Local Authorities' final consumption	33.3	47.4	49.9	C
plus Gross investment expenditure	74.0	95.4	94.7	D
plus Value of physical increase in stocks and work in progress	1.3	(5.3)	(0.2)	E
equals TOTAL DOMESTIC SPENDING	428.1	579.7	638.6	F
plus The value of exports of goods and services	107.0	135.1	158.0	G
equals TOTAL FINAL EXPENDITURE	535.1	714.8	796.6	H
less Imports of goods and services	(111.8)	(140.4)	(166.2)	I
equals GROSS DOMESTIC PRODUCT AT MARKET PRICES ('money GDP')	423.3	574.4	630.4	J
minus Taxes on expenditure (VAT & excise)	69.0	(83.0)	(91.3)	K
plus subsidies	6.1	5.8	7.4	
equals GROSS DOMESTIC PRODUCT AT FACTOR COST	360.4	497.2	546.5	L
plus Net property income from abroad	3.7	0.3	3.0	M
equals GROSS NATIONAL PRODUCT AT FACTOR COST	364.1	497.5	549.5	N
less depreciation allowance at 15% (called capital consumption)	48.1	(63.3)	(65.0)	O
equals NATIONAL INCOME	316.0	434.2	484.5	P

I   This figure is subtracted to discover the value of domestic product as distinct from the sum of total spending.

J   Money GDP is becoming more popular as a measure of economic activity in current price terms. Also known as NOMINAL GDP.

K   This is the 'factor cost adjustment'. Money GDP can be misleading because it includes expenditure taxes and subsidies. These are excluded here to give a value of GDP in terms of resources used.

L   This is the most commonly used measure of a western nation's domestic output. Factor cost means the cost of land, labour and capital used in production of goods and services.

M   Countries such as the UK have extensive investments overseas which result in a flow of interest, profits and dividends. Also, there is an outflow from the UK to overseas residents. This item is the net figure. It is misleading, it refers to the ownerships of assets not just homes.

N   This figure shows the value of our gross national output from all sources.

O   All plant and equipment wears out. Here an allowance is made for this.

P   The UK national income in current prices.

Q   Goods held in stock will usually appreciate over a year (particularly if the inflation rate is higher). The stock appreciation figures adjusts for this. It is not the same as (E), which measures the physical movement in stocks and work in progress.

R   This figure should be the same as (L) but errors and omissions result in a discrepancy.

S   The fiddle factor – used to balance the books. In the original estimates it was £7.9Bn for 1987, subsequently revised to zero.

T   This approximates the amount paid in interest by UK companies.

U   This is an estimate of what people would earn if they rented their homes.

V   This is an allowance for the capital assets consumed by non-trading entities.

Each person's expenditure is another person's income. Therefore, Gross Domestic Product can be measured by adding up the incomes earned in the economy, as follows:

	£ billion 1987	£ billion 1991	£ billion 1993	Refer to:
Income from employment	229.8	329.8	352.8	
plus gross trading profits of companies	59.2	60.6	73.3	
plus gross trading profits of public corporations	6.8	3.1	3.4	
plus gross trading profits of general government enterprises	(0.07)	(0.1)	0.3	
plus income from self employment and rents	66.2	101.6	114.1	
plus capital consumption	3.3	4.4	3.9	V
equals TOTAL DOMESTIC INCOME	365.3	499.4	547.8	
less stock appreciation	(4.7)	(2.8)	(2.3)	Q
Equals GROSS DOMESTIC PRODUCT, INCOME BASED	360.5	497.0	545.5	R
less residual error	–	–	1.0	S
equals GROSS DOMESTIC PRODUCT AT FACTOR COST (income method)	360.5	497.0	546.5	L
equals GROSS DOMESTIC PRODUCT AT FACTOR COST (expenditure method) as calculated (on previous page)	360.5	497.0	546.5	L

Finally, if Gross Domestic Product is the final value of goods and services sold, then it must be calculable by summing the contributions to final value made by each industry in the economy.

This is difficult to do, because of the problem of double counting. Consider the example of a bar of steel which is sold to a firm which then machines it to produce a car component, which is then part of a car and sold to the final consumer. Summing the value of output at each stage would count the steel bar three times. To avoid double counting, the value added from each firm is calculated.

Measuring GDP by summing the value of sector output, after adjusting for double counting. This is the sector contribution.

	£billion 1987	£billion 1991	£billion 1993	Refer to:
Agriculture, forestry and fishing	6.9	8.7	10.3	
Energy and water supply	25.2	28.2	26.0	
Manufacturing	82.8	104.2	118.2	
Construction	24.0	33.6	29.2	
Distribution, hotels & catering, repairs	50.5	73.0	78.3	
Transport and communication	25.9	34.7	46.2	
Banking, Finance, insurance business services and leasing	59.5	88.1	93.0	
Ownership of dwellings: rent	20.9	34.8	41.0	U
Public admin., natural defence and compulsory social security	24.9	34.7	38.1	
Education and health	33.1	49.3	57.4	
Other services	23.3	33.9	31.2	
	374.5			
Less stock appreciation	(4.7)	(2.8)	(2.3)	Q
Less adjustment for financial services	(16.9)	(27.1)	(23.7)	T
	349.2	355.3		R
Residual error	**5.2**	(3.7)	0.3	S
GROSS DOMEST IC PRODUCT AT FACTOR COST	**360.5**	497	546.1	L

What do the estimates for GDP tell us?

They do not give the full picture of economic activity within an economy. Work done but not paid for (e.g. housewife activity) or vegetables grown for own consumption or DIY, is not measured. Therefore the GDP figures understate to a large extent what is physically produced and consumed.

The output measures give a good indication of the importance of each industry sector and when one year is compared to another, the changing structure of an economy can be tracked.

In 1987, 1991 and 1993 the main percentage of contributions to United Kingdom GDP were as follows:

	1987 %	1991 %	1993 %
Manufacturing	21.9	19.9	21.7
Banking, insurance and leasing	15.8	16.8	16.1
Distribution, hotels, catering and repairs	13.4	13.9	13.4
Education and health	8.7	9.4	10.0
Transport and communication	6.8	6.6	8.1
Public Admin, defence and social support	6.6	6.6	6.6
Energy and water supply	6.6	5.3	4.5
Construction	6.3	6.4	5.9
Other services	6.1	6.4	5.4
Property ownership	5.5	6.4	7.2
Agriculture, forestry and fishing	1.8	1.6	1.8
Totals	99.3	99.3	100.7

The table shows that one third of the economy is concerned with making things; the remaining two thirds are concerned with distributing, selling and servicing the output of this sector.

The GDP deflator

GDP is measured at current prices. So the numbers are higher not only because of volume of goods sold but because of prices rising. To obtain a measure of the volume change in GDP, the current price figures must be adjusted for inflation. The adjustment uses a relevant price index such as the Retail Price Index or Producers Price Index. Each of the component series of GDP is adjusted in this way. Then they are summarized, and the total is divided into GDP at current prices. The result is the GDP deflator which is a measure of inflation in GDP, weighted by its components.

$$\text{GDP deflator} = \frac{\text{GDP at current prices}}{\text{GDP at constant prices}}$$

A Note on index numbers

A base weighted index is a weighted average. Each item is weighted (i.e. given a proportion of the whole – the sum of the weights is one) to reflect its relative importance to the purchaser. For example, assume that industry spends 20% of its income on fuel and 80% on materials. The Base year January 1990 is 100; the weights are 0.20 and 0.80.

	A Fuel	B Materials	C Total
weights	0.20	0.80	100
Jan 1990	100	100	100
Jan 1991	103	105.5	105.0
Jan 1992	108	117.4	115.5

Column C = (column A x 0.20) + (column B x 0.80).

The weights are assigned at the start; rebasing just means a new period equals 100 and every number is divided by the value of the new base.

The Producer Price Index

This index is calculated from the price movements of 10,000 separate items; mostly materials and products purchased and manufactured by UK industry. It is a base weighted index. Rebasing takes place every five years. The index relates to average price movements each month; VAT is excluded but excise duty is included.

This index replaced the wholesale price index in 1983. It is used to give an indication of 'core' inflation.

The Retail Price Index in a nutshell

The RPI measures the overall change in the prices of things people buy, including services like travel and entertainment as well as goods from shops. Only savings and income tax are left out. Some things are more important than others in terms of the amount of money spent on them and this is allowed for in the index. For example, a given percentage increase in the price of bread has about four times the effect of a similar increase in the price of butter. The change in the index is therefore an average of the individual price changes for practically all goods and services, with more weight being given to those items on which people spend most.

The Retail Price Index is not a *cost of living* index although it is called one: nor does it measure what people have to spend on necessities in order to stay alive. However, it does measure price changes and thus provides an indication of what people would need to spend each month so as to repurchase the things they chose to buy at the beginning of the year. It can therefore be regarded as a good approximation to a change in the cost of living.

The index is an accurate measure of price changes across the whole country. It is compiled from about 130,000 separate price quotations collected each month, mainly by personal visits to shops. The way it is constructed is overseen by an independent advisory committee on which consumers, retailers, employers and employees are all represented.

The RPI can be used to check whether take-home pay (after tax and national insurance) has kept pace with prices. If take-home pay increases by more than the index over a certain period (say a year) then people will be better off at the end of the period than at the start, in the sense that they will be able to buy more goods and services with their money.

The RPI reflects the experience of the average household. It does not apply precisely to any one family or person but is broadly correct for the great majority of households and is the best available indicator of inflation for most people.

International comparisons

The GDP estimates are in local currency. International Comparisons of GDP are often misleading; because countries are at different stages of their economic development, and their currencies have different relative values. One approach is to translate the figures using purchasing power parities or PPP.

This method bases prices in each country in a single currency (usually the dollar) in such a way that $1 will purchase the same quantity in each country.

To illustrate, take the example of the UK and Australia. In 1990, Australia's GDP was $294.1 Bn at current prices and current exchange rates. Per person it was $17,215. The UK's GDP was $975.1 at current prices and current exchange rates; per person $16,985. On a PPP basis, Australia is $15,900 per person and the UK $15,882, per person.

On a current exchange rate basis, Australia is 1.3% richer per person but on a PPP basis, only 0.1% richer.

Clearly there are problems when we use estimates in currencies the value of which changes in, and between, countries.

Perhaps a better indication is the per thousand approach. To enable a meaningful comparison; cars, telephones, TVs, Doctors and infant mortality per 1000 people can be used.

Again taking Australia and the UK, compared with the USA.

	Australia	UK	USA
Cars per 1000	570	449	748
Telephones per 1000	550	524	650
TVs per 1000	217	435	812
Doctors	2.3	1.4	2.3
Infant deaths	8.2	7.9	9.2

On this basis, Australia enjoys a higher standard of living than the UK; but neither country can match the USA for cars, TVs and doctors, although both beat the USA on infant mortality.

These figures give only a vague indication of the quality of life. They don't show happiness, contentment, fulfilment, feeling of security, living space, quality of services and food. They do not indicate levels of pollution or resources depletion.

The difference between GDP and GNP

GDP at market prices is the sum of the final value of goods and services sold less the value of imports of goods and services.

GNP at market prices is the sum of the final value of goods and services sold less the value of imports of goods and services plus net property income from abroad.

Property income is a flow of interest, profits and dividends from a country's ownership of assets overseas. Net property income is the inflow from overseas less the amount paid to people overseas who own assets in the domestic system.

The flow is estimated and recorded in the invisibles section on the current account of the balance of payments.

As a country like the UK attracts more inward investment, then the net contribution is likely to fall in the future. For example, in 1987 net property income was £3.7 Billion; in 1991, it was a mere £0.3 Billion.

This is because the stream of earnings to overseas investors will increase steadily as their UK investments pay dividends.

3 What causes changes in the level of GDP?

GDP is measured in money values. If there is inflation, the money value of GDP will change and this may disguise volume changes. Assume that there is no inflation, therefore the value of money is constant from one year to the next. Under this assumption changes in money GDP are equal to changes in real GDP.

The economy is a set of integrated individual markets. GDP measures the final value of goods and services sold in each market. Markets are driven by people, who possess 'animal spirits'. People acting individually or collectively (as corporate boards or pension fund managers) have emotions and expectations. These determine one of the key decisions in the system, whether to save or spend current income and whether to spend on investment (the purchase of land, plant equipment or technology which increases future income flows) or consumption (the purchase of any item which has no impact on future income flows).

Saving from current income is a withdrawal from the flow of spending in and between markets, and with a time lag (and without compensatory injection) reduces the flow of GDP.

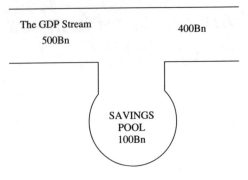

Imports represent expenditure on goods and services imported from overseas. The income flows into another economy, reducing the flow in the domestic economy.

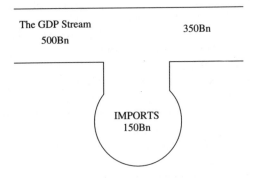

Taxation (not matched by Government spending) is also a withdrawal:

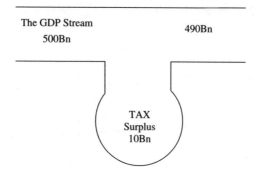

There are three withdrawals:

SAVINGS
IMPORTS
TAXATION

Withdrawals is a sum of money taken from the main flow of the system. However, there are also three main items of expenditure into the GDP stream called injections. An injection is a sum of money spent in the main flow of the system.

Investment spending is an injection:

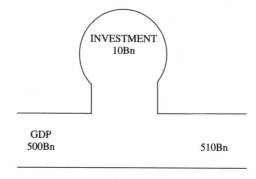

Exports are an injection:

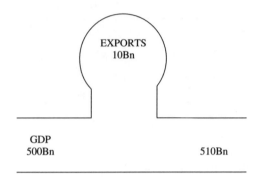

Government spending is an injection:

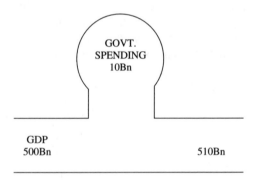

The complete system is in balance when the amount withdrawn is simultaneously matched by the amount injected:

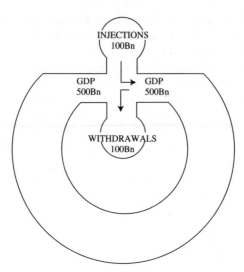

If the level of withdrawals is greater than the level of injections, the GDP stream gets smaller:

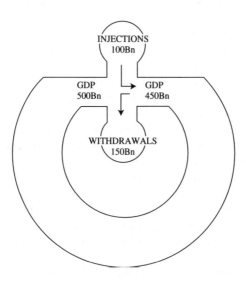

In the model so far we have likened the system to a stream with injections into the stream and withdrawals from the stream.

This is over simplistic.

The GDP figures are a snapshot of the system taken at a single point in time. If in year one GDP is £500 Bn but the next year it is £600 Bn and there has been no inflation, what is of interest is how the economy grew. What forces were at work? GDP movements are determined by the amount of money in the economy and the number of times it gets spent by the players in individual markets.

NB: If the structure of the economy is unchanged then an increase in spending will be reflected in a pro rata increase in GDP.

THE MONEY GO ROUND

You may recall in Chapter 1 I mentioned the difference between the *total value* of *transactions* and the *value* of *economic activity*.

The total value of transactions is 42× the value of economic activity in the UK.

The value of economic activity is estimated by the GDP figures. Assuming no change in the structure of the economy, i.e. the way in which added value is produced, then an increase in the amount of money in the system will increase both the value of transactions and the value of economic activity pro rata. If some unit of money went round the system further, it would finance more transactions and more GDP.

A ten pound note spent 30 times in a year can finance £300 worth of transactions. If spent 60 times, it can finance £600 worth of transactions.

Total spending by definition is the amount of money multiplied by the number of times it gets spent, (known as the velocity of money).

If an extra £10 is injected into the system, and the velocity is 30, then it will finance an extra £300 worth of transactions.

Velocity is calculated by taking GDP at market prices and dividing it by the amount of money.

In 1994 GDP was £668 Bn, the amount of money in cash was £23 Bn.

Velocity is therefore 668 ÷ 23 = 29×.

An extra ten pounds would finance £290 worth of transactions. (Because we are using GDP figures £290 represents added value). If for some reason people decided to save part of the £10, then less would be spent, the value of transactions would be lower, and velocity can be said to have fallen.

e.g. GDP £600 Bn ÷ 23 Bn = 26×.

The extra ten pounds is financing only £260 pounds worth of transactions.

We can conclude that both the amount of money and the rate at which it circulates are important drivers of GDP at market prices.

If the amount of money increases, velocity constant, nominal GDP goes up. If the amount of money is constant, velocity goes up, nominal GDP goes up or some combination of the two.

Both the amount of money and its velocity are determined by behaviour; the amount of money by the domestic banking system, and its velocity by individuals' and companys' decisions to spend or save. It is a complex set of inter-relationships and this section of the book is designed to get to the fundamentals.

We are looking at a flow of spending between people in the system and what causes changes in the level of the flow. Clearly the relationships between injections and withdrawals will reflect both the level and the rate of flow.

A key concept is the multiplier. The multiplier effect is the result of a small change in spending behaviour in one part of the system washing through the whole system as individuals react to changing circumstances. Bearing in mind that one man's expenditure is another man's income, it can easily be recognized that a small uncritical change in one part of the system causes the whole system to change. It is a bit like throwing a stone into a still pond, there is an initial splash and then the shock waves spread across the whole pond and get larger, such that the whole pond is disturbed, even though the stone fell into one part of it. But eventually the waves become less and less powerful and the pond becomes still again.

For economists a still pond is one in equilibrium. Equilibrium means unchanging: economies are never in equilibrium, because people are always throwing stones, and there are always multiplier effects.

In summary:

if INJECTIONS > WITHDRAWALS	expansions in spending with a multiplier effect
if INJECTIONS = WITHDRAWALS	constant spending no multiplier
if INJECTIONS < WITHDRAWALS	contraction in spending with a downward multiplier effect

We spend money in exchange for goods and services. Prices are determined by the interaction of willing buyers and sellers. Prices will rise if there are more willing buyers than sellers.

For the economy as a whole if total spending exceeds the ability of producers to supply they will raise their selling prices, and we have inflation. Inflation is an increase in the general level of prices through time.

So for any economy it is important to consider spending levels in relation to capacity.

The demand side of the economy is spending, the supply side is capacity.

So far we have described changes on the demand or spending side. But it is important to understand the supply side.

The supply side is the economy's ability to produce goods and services.

Each economy has so much installed capacity or productive potential. This is determined by the size, type, and skills of the labour force; the infrastructure (i.e. roads, telecoms, sewerage and electricity supplies); the availability of local raw materials; the level of technology embodied in the existing plant equipment and buildings.

It is also determined by the cultural characteristics of the population and their value systems. In particular their attitude to productivity, quality and efficiency.

If the economy were fully employed (factories, people and infrastructure) then a certain level of output would be produced.

Position A

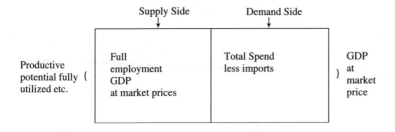

Here the economy is balanced at full employment of productive potential. Assume too that the value of imports is identical to the value of exports (there is a balance on the External Account).

Assume there is no inflation.

Now assume the value of imports exceeds the value of exports, all other things held constant. There will be spare capacity and unemployment.

Position B

unused capacity	lost to imports
GDP at market prices	TOTAL SPEND less imports

Now assume that domestic producers increase their sales abroad (the value of exports go up) but the value of imports remain unchanged and now equals the value of exports.

Position C

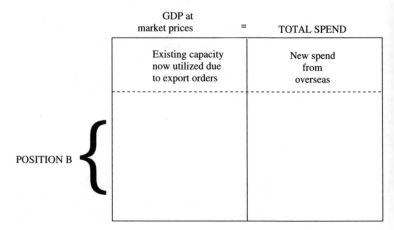

We return to Position A. The economy has a balance of imports and exports, full employment of productive potential and stable prices.

We are comparing one position with another. We are not discussing how the system moves from one position to the other, i.e. the multiplier effect.

Position D

Now assume that all producers of goods and services decide to raise their prices by 10%, (and their wages and dividends) but

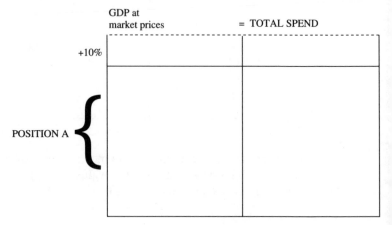

keeping the volume of output the same as before. Also assume the value of imports still equals the value of exports.

There is inflation, the value of output is up 10%, the volume of spending is up 10%. The volume of goods and services remains the same. Real GDP is unchanged, nominal GDP is up 10%. In money terms there has been a 10% increase. In fact the standard of living is unchanged, the same number of people are producing the same number of goods and services as before.

Position E

Assume an economy with nearly full employment with a balance on the external account and stable prices. Now assume a surge in investment spending

unused capacity	INCREASE IN INVESTMENT SPEND
GDP at market prices	TOTAL SPEND

Total spend rises above available output for a period of time, because the increase in spend is on capacity creation which is not yet producing saleable output. There is a gap between money demand (total spend) and available supply. In a market system this gap (the inflationary gap) gets filled by a combination of rising prices and increased imports.

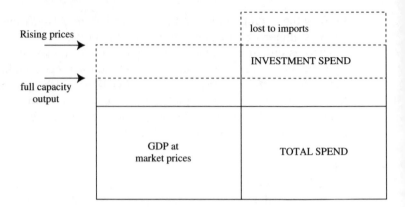

The inflationary gap is filled by rising prices. The economy now has rising prices, increased investment spending, falling unemployment and growth.

Position F

Assume that producers raise prices by 10% and wages by 10%, but that simultaneously producers and consumers increase their saving. This saving is not offset by investment spending.

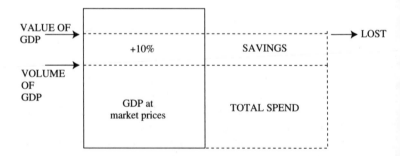

Here the price of output is up 10%, the volume of output remains the same. This is known as stagflation. Under some circumstances, the volume of GDP can fall, and the value increase, especially if simultaneously producers and income earners raise their prices but reduce their output. This is known as 'slumpflation'. A period of inflation and reductions in real economic activity.

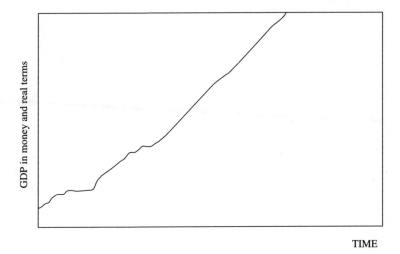

Figure 3.1 A balanced growth economy. In this diagram, money and real GDP are equal. There is no inflation.

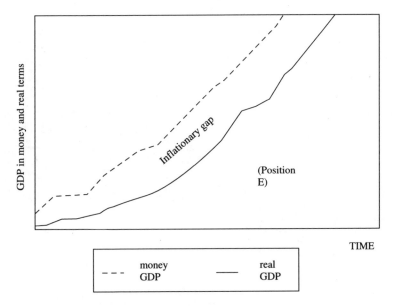

Figure 3.2 An unbalanced growth economy.

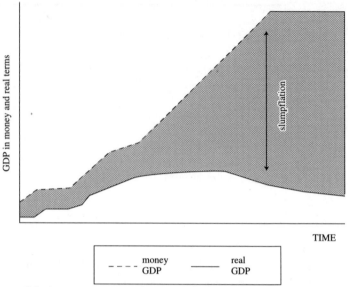

Figure 3.3 An economy experiencing inflation and simultaneously falling output (known as slumpflation)

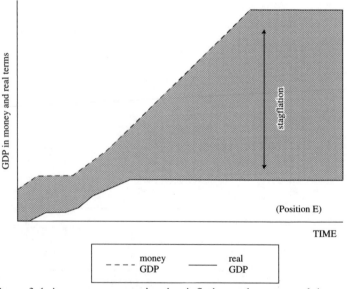

Figure 3.4 An economy experiencing inflation and zero growth in output (known as stagflation)

CHAPTER SUMMARY

- Economic activity is the result of exchange between individuals. Any exchange will change income.
- GDP measures the extent to which an economic system has added value. It does not measure all economic activity; only that which adds value.
- Wealth and income are different. Wealth is an increase in the physical stock of things which is the result of production, which adds value, which creates incomes and GDP.
- GDP can be estimated in three different ways: by summing total incomes; by summing the value of final sales; by summing the value of final output.
- Because we measure activity in nominal (money) terms, any change in the value of money has to be accounted for by deflating the nominal figures for GDP. International comparisons are difficult to make for the same reason; nominal values are in differing currencies.
- The flow of spending in the economy changes as a result of imbalances between injections and withdrawals. This is the main source of instability. Economies can experience inflation, slumpflation and stagflation. A balanced growth economy is unusual.

4 Economic policy and a dynamic system: the business cycle

Have you ever met someone who is totally satisfied with their material well being? I haven't. People always want more things, or better things: Even those who say they are not materialistic demand better education, more libraries, better public transport, more help for the elderly, a modern health care system, vibrant arts in the community programmes, and environmental protection technology.

All products or services consume material and human resources. People expect their country to be run in such a way that their wants and needs are met.

In democracies Governments see their primary aim is to enable the nation to increase its living standards each year. They call this economic growth. Another way of looking at it is to say that the task of Government is to ensure value added per person grows year on year.

The first aim of economic policy is to produce growth.

The fundamental purpose of economic activity is to reduce scarcity: the gap between what people desire and what they currently have.

In a market economy, if there is a mismatch between the rate of growth in the total spend and the ability of the system to supply goods and services, then prices in general increase. There is inflation. A low and stable rate of inflation, say 2% per annum is not a problem (assuming competitor nations have the same rate of inflation), unless many of the inhabitants are on fixed incomes. But a variable rate of inflation is a problem. If the rate of inflation in year 1 is 5%, year II 12% and year III 22% and these rates were not expected, then many participants in the economy will find their personal and business plans are inappropriate or misleading. This leads to confusion, which dislocates the system.

The second aim of policy is to ensure a stable price level (not necessarily zero – a low, but *stable* inflation rate is usually acceptable).

The third aim of economic policy is to ensure that resources are fully employed. In a world of scarcity unemployed or under-utilized resources is a waste. Real GDP per person is lower than it otherwise would be. It is desirable to run the economy as near as possible to full employment.

The fourth aim of economic policy is to ensure that a country's trading surplus or deficit with the rest of the world is not too large measured as a percentage of GDP. The world is a closed system, one country's surplus must be another's deficit, so Governments try to obtain a rough balance on the external account.

THE BALANCE BETWEEN INJECTIONS AND WITHDRAWALS

In any market economy, relative prices are always shifting and these movements provide signals to the players in the system.

The rate of interest is the price of money for investment. It is also the return to savers. The rate of interest should always move to equate savings and investment.

The exchange rate is the value of one country's currency in terms of another. The exchange rate is determined by market forces and should move to always equalize the demand for currency and the supply of that currency. Changes in currency values change the relative prices of internationally traded goods, which in turn can cause volume to change.

In principle the exchange rate should move to match the value of imports with the value of exports.

The Government can determine the structure of taxation. The level of GDP and its rate of change will determine the yield.

The Government can plan its own level of spending, but the level and rate of change in GDP will determine the amount actually spent.

WITHDRAWALS   INJECTIONS

The rate of interest

SAVINGS	INVESTMENT

The exchange rate   } MONETARY POLICY

IMPORTS	EXPORTS

TAXATION	GOVERMENT SPENDING

} FISCAL POLICY

If the sum of withdrawals is exactly matched by the sum of injections the economy is stable. Economic instability is the result of an imbalance between withdrawals and injections.

If withdrawals exceed injections for a period then the economy will contract, if injections exceed withdrawals the economy will expand. Economic instability is the norm, because injections are seldom, if ever matched by withdrawals, this is because the people who save in an economy are different from those who invest.

Growth is a form of instability, Injections > Withdrawals

Recession is a form of instability, Injections < Withdrawals

Stagnation = stable = Injections ≡ Withdrawals

Governments like to deliver growth, but at a rate which can be sustained without inflation or a balance of payments deficit.

Governments have objectives

In a democracy the overriding objective is to gain or maintain power. 'Getting the economy right' is seen as essential for electoral success. Governments set broad economic objectives which constitute getting the economy right.

Economic objectives:

- stable prices
- economic growth
- 'fuller' employment
- a balance on the external account

Policy actions
- Monetary
- Fiscal

Instruments

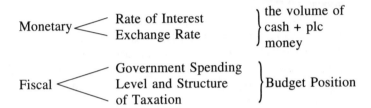

Monetary — Rate of Interest / Exchange Rate } the volume of cash + plc money

Fiscal — Government Spending / Level and Structure of Taxation } Budget Position

Targets

A government will have explicit or implicit targets to guide its policy actions. An example could be 2.5% real growth per annum with 3% inflation rate per annum and not more than 10% unemployment.

Also the balance of payments on current account to have a surplus or deficit not to exceed 1% of GDP.

In a market economy it is not possible to deliver continuously on all four economic objectives (the dynamics of the multiplier and investment accelerator (see Chapter 3) make it impossible). So Government is forced to order them in importance as perceived by the electorate. This order changes through time and so therefore does economic policy. The timing of elections is crucial as is getting 'the economy right' to win an election.

Scenario A

For the past three years assume the government has been emphasizing growth, job creation and a reduction in unemployment. To achieve this they have had expansionary fiscal policy (government spending > tax receipts) and an expansionary monetary policy (PLC money – see Chapter 5 – has been expanding rapidly as the result of lower interest rates and the level of investment spending > level of saving).

Multiplier effects are working through all sectors of the economic system. This is reflected in the fact that the majority of firms are exceeding their sales forecasts, individuals are enjoying higher than expected incomes from employment, and dividends. Bank lending is increasing as firms and individuals feel confident that they can easily finance their increased borrowings (PLC money is expanding; more on this later).

As the economy moves towards full employment, bottlenecks appear on the supply side.

Suppliers begin quoting longer delivery dates and higher prices. Manufacturers find that it is difficult to attract skilled labour unless the wages offered are well above the current levels. As poaching of skilled labour intensifies, the wages paid to this group increase rapidly. Productivity growth slows because plant is operating at capacity with wage pressures. Firms maintain or grow their margins by raising their prices above the retail price index. These feed through almost directly to the bottom line and return on capital employed increases.

The manufacturers key ratios are:

$$\text{MARGIN} \quad \times \quad \text{ASSET UTILIZATION} = \quad \text{ROCE}$$

$$\frac{\text{Profit}}{\text{Sales}} \quad \times \quad \frac{\text{Sales}}{\text{Assets}} \quad = \quad \frac{\text{Return on Capital}}{\text{Employed}}$$

Margins and asset utilization are both improving, so ROCE is rising.

Assume that the government notices that producer prices are moving upwards, and it wishes to slow the economy down to limit the extent of overheating.

It decides to raise interest rates (i.e. tighten monetary policy).

Such is the level of confidence about future sales and margins, the higher rate of interest (up 2%) makes little difference.

After a time lag, interest rates go up another 2%, and then after another time lag the multiplier begins to work in reverse, leading to a rapid slow down in sales, profits and return on capital employed, and after another time lag, price increases slow down.

How does this work?

A manufacturing business consists of people, capital plant, equipment, materials and finished product. The business exists to add value to raw materials. Each year or quarter the business team will formalize their view of the future. The plan in essence will have the following components:

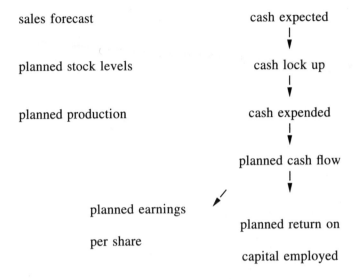

sales forecast

planned stock levels

planned production

planned earnings

per share

cash expected

cash lock up

cash expended

planned cash flow

planned return on

capital employed

The business is a coalition of individuals with conflicting interests. Sales and marketing people will wish to maximize volume and margin – they are also optimistic as a general rule.

Finance people wish to achieve planned return and growth in earnings per share and also ensure that the balance sheet and profit and loss account match the expectations of the city analysts. The finance people will know the difference between cash (liquidity) and profit.

The production side of the business will be concerned with efficient plant utilization and cost minimization (not profit maximization, or sales revenue maximization).

To achieve their objectives production want long steady manufacturing runs. There will be cost penalties if more than planned is required (extensive overtime working) or less than planned is required (low overhead recovery).

We start with the sales forecast, produced by sales and marketing people.

They will look at the historic pattern of sales and plot them to obtain a trend line.

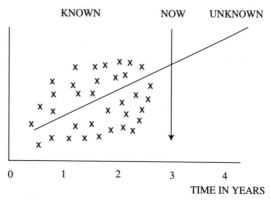

Figure 4.1 Sales forecast

There will be strong behavioural reasons why sales and marketing will choose a forecast which is around, if not on, the sales trend.

This forecast will be translated into a stock budget (custom and practice requires so many days sales in stock) for approval by finance (because stock equals cash lock up) and then the aggregated figures will become the production plan.

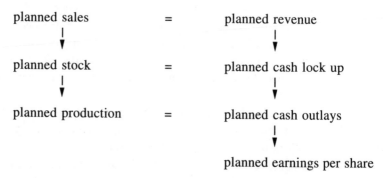

Because of higher than expected interest rates, actual sales in the first quarter are below planned, say down 2%.

The quarterly sales review meeting talk in terms of 'blips' which have an explanation. A decision is taken to leave the production schedules alone (to the great relief of the production manager) and allow stocks to build (OK for as long as the stock build is within budget).

At the end of the second quarter sales have not improved as hoped for. Indeed the variance (actual compared to plan) is now running at 5%. Stocks are rising fast (variance + 15% on plan) and the finance director is becoming concerned with 'cash lock up' and company liquidity (i.e. the rate of cash generation from sales is only slightly ahead of cash outflow on overheads, wages and materials).

By the end of the third quarter things have worsened. Sales variance is now minus 10%, stock variance +25% and there is some concern for the financial position (i.e. liquidity of the business. It has increased its short term borrowings to finance stocks at 3% above base rate. This cuts the net profit, and also increases gearing (debt to equity).

The finance director's main concern is over the deteriorating balance sheet, and what could be done to produce a year end balance sheet which would not cause adverse city comment and brokers 'sell' suggestions.

The decision is taken to generate and conserve cash as quickly as possible by reducing stocks and cutting all 'unnecessary' expenditure. The training budget is cut, advertising and promotion is cut, R & D is cut, but the biggest saving comes from cutting production and laying off the workforce.

```
Destocking = stocks into cash
achieved by
cutting the rate of PRODUCTION
below the current rate of SALES
```

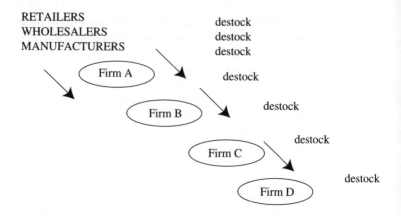

As firms destock the multiplier works in reverse. The velocity of money falls as companies hang on to cash.

The process takes about 24 months before stocks throughout the economy are at a level which companies find acceptable. At this point production stops falling.

The process of destocking is a withdrawal from the system. Goods are sold for cash which is not passed on in the form of wages or investment spending. Instead it is used to reduce the firm's borrowing. If the bank is also going liquid the cash will sit in its accounts and not underpin an expansion of PLC money.

In terms of our model, destocking is

SAVINGS > INVESTMENT

and the multiplier effect is firm A cutting orders from firm B who cuts orders from firm C and so on.

Take a look at the graph in Figure 4.2. It shows that in 1979 stocks and work in progress fell by £3.4 billion.

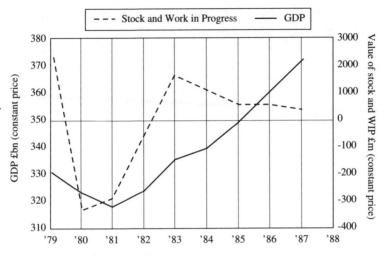

Figure 4.2 UK GDP growth and change in stocks

Associated with this was a 15% reduction in orders for the engineering industry, an 18% reduction in orders for the construction industry and a 14% reduction in car production. Overall production fell by 8%.

In the UK one of the reasons why stocks in 1979 were high in relation to sales is the tax benefit. In 1975 Dennis Healey introduced a scheme which allowed firms to claim full tax relief on the increase in value of stocks. At a time of negative real interest rates (i.e. inflation is higher than the interest rate) it is tax efficient for firms to build stocks, financed by borrowing, and claim tax relief. This made holding stock as attractive as cash in the bank.

In 1979 it was announced that the scheme would be phased out over the next five years.

By 1984 there was no tax advantage in holding stocks, and real interest rates were positive.

From 1984 onwards, UK companies have operated with lower stock-output ratios than previously. In addition, improvements in technology (such as EPOS in retail outlets and the shift to superstores) have achieved economies of scale in stockholding.

A recession is caused by cash conservation by means of destocking, postponing investment plans and cutting all unnecessary expenditure.

But the start point is the problem of mismatch between company plans and actual events.

If companies have experienced increasing sales, incomes and business opportunities, they generally are confident that based on the recent past, things will get even better.

However, there are always shocks to the system, which prompt a rapid change in expectations.

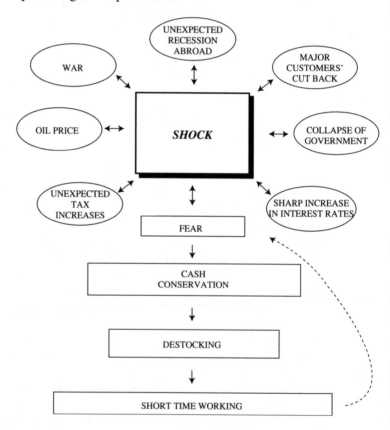

Recessions end because with the passage of time people get used to their changed circumstances and their confidence stops declining. The fear factor reduces and with it the desire to conserve cash. Simultaneously most man-made goods are wearing out. Cars, washing machines, carpets, the lawn mower and the hoover need replacing. The house needs essential repairs. In the factory, plant and equipment reach the end of their useful life. For the distribution companies the fleet of trucks needs replacing and so on.

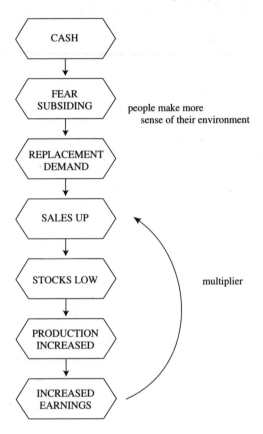

BUSINESS STOCKS

Cleaned out – reproduced from the Economist September 1992

Before America slipped into recession last year, most economists argued that the better methods of stock (inventory) control adopted by businesses over the past decade would prevent a repeat of the big swings in stocks seen in the past – and so help to prevent recession. Businessmen were clearly not listening: they have been slashing their stocks almost as aggressively as in previous downturns.

Because firms hold stocks – raw materials, work in progress and finished goods – in order to smooth out their production, stocks tend to be the most volatile bit of GNP. Destocking has, on average, accounted for three-quarters of the total fall in GNP in the past six recessions. Firms have traditionally been caught out by the fall in sales and kept churning out widgets long after customers stop buying them. The resulting increase in stocks has later forced companies to slash output, magnifying the effect of the original decline in sales and often turning slow-down into slump.

This time, however, things were supposed to be different. American firms entered the recession with lower stocks than usual – equivalent to 1.45 months of sales, compared with 1.6 at the start of the 1981–82 recession. This was partly because high real interest rates had encouraged firms to keep stock levels down. Also, the use of computers and just-in-time production techniques has reduced the required level of stocks for any given level of demand by shortening the time between when raw materials enter the factory and when finished goods leave it.

The new techniques were meant to allow firms to match production more closely to demand and so ensure smaller fluctuations in stocks than in the past. This, argued economists, would smooth out the business cycle. The jury is still out, but the preliminary evidence hardly suggests that the stock cycle has been tamed. American businesses have cut their stocks in the past 12 months by almost as much as the average in previous recessions. The turnaround from stockbuilding to destocking accounted for two-thirds of the total drop in GNP since the third quarter of last year.

It was easy to fine-tune stocks when the economy was growing steadily, but firms still seem to have been caught out by the recession. Have the new stock-control techniques failed their first test?

One explanation is that the decline in stocks says more about the number of firms that have not introduced better stock control than about those which have. Surveys suggest that only 15–20% of manufacturing firms currently use just-in-time methods. It is most common among car and machinery manufacturers, such as Ford, GM, Xerox and Hewlett Packard, which have typically been able to reduce stocks by half or more over the past decade.

But many firms claiming to have just-in-time systems have in fact done little more than transfer stocks to their suppliers. Another factor is that, whereas the ratio of manufacturing stocks to sales fell during the 1980s, retailers and wholesalers were less successful in controlling stock. Retailers' stocks rose quite sharply relative to sales, despite the millions of dollars they invested in product-scanners and computers to give them up-to-the-minute information on sales and stocks. One reason is that manufacturers tried to shift some of the burden of carrying stocks on to retailers by offering discounts to those willing to carry larger stocks. A bigger factor was the rapid growth in the number of shops – by 2.5% a year between 1982 and 1987, compared with an annual 0.5% in the previous 20 years.

There is some compensation for the failure of just-in-time to reduce the swings in stock levels: firms' aggressive destocking in the past three quarters could itself provide a springboard for recovery. If the level of stocks simply remains unchanged in the current quarter, and everything else stays the same, then factories will begin to churn out more to meet orders rather than simply shifting goods from the warehouse. That, by itself, would boost GNP by an annualized 2.7%. Wow!

The graph in Figure 4.3 shows the behaviour of consumer spending split between non-durables and durables. The figures

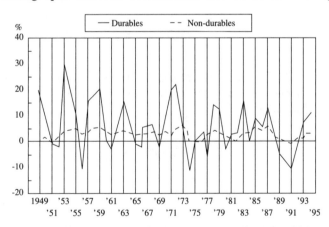

Figure 4.3 Expenditure on durables and non-durables 1949–95 expressed as a % of previous years level of spending on these items.
Source: Lombard Street Research.

are inflation adjusted. As can be seen, the change in the level of durable spending is much greater than for non durable.

It is impossible to forecast exactly when changes will take place. But we know it will always happen. Consumer durable spend is 6% of GDP. This is only a couple of points less than the value of UK Construction industry output.

The swing is the key. It makes it a third as powerful as non-durables spending which is fifty nine percent of GDP. The effect is multiplied by company stockbuilding behaviour. Taken together these are the major source of instability for all mature economies. Government can moderate but not eradicate this effect. There is no such thing as a stable market economy.

THE INCOMES MULTIPLIER AND THE INVESTMENT ACCELERATOR

The incomes multiplier is driven by the fact that one person's expenditure is another's income. So ten pounds of new spending generates incomes which are a multiple of its value. Assuming no tax or imports withdrawals and that each person in the economy saved 10% of their income then the value of the multiplier is ten. This is calculated by taking the reciprocal of the savings rate.

$$\text{Multiplier} = \frac{1}{0.1} = 10$$

This suggests that an extra £10 spent will in time generate £100 of new incomes. If people decided to save 20% of their current income then

$$\text{Multiplier} = \frac{1}{0.2} = 5$$

The extra £10 spent will generate only £50 of new incomes.

In a complex, open economy such as the UK, there are considerable withdrawals i.e. losses to tax, saving and imports.

What is called the GDP multiplier is more complex and is

$$\frac{1}{\% \text{ taken in tax, } + \% \text{ spent on imports } + \% \text{ saved}}$$

It is estimated by the UK Treasury to have a value of 1.33. For every extra £10 spent, about £7.50 is lost to tax, savings and imports.

$$\text{The GDP Multiplier} = \frac{1}{0.75} = 1.33$$

The arithmetic suggests that £10 extra spending will eventually generate £13.30 of new incomes.

So the value of the GDP multiplier will fall if the population saves more, imports more or pay more taxes per capita (not offset by an equivalent increase in Government spending).

The investment accelerator

The principle is simple. A manufacturer will estimate sales before building a factory and filling it with equipment. He will try and match expected sales with capacity. If actual sales are greater than expected, the factory and its equipment will be worked more intensively e.g. by double shift working. If sales continue to grow faster than expected and, despite double shift working, orders are lost due to the inability to supply, then it is likely that new capacity will be ordered. A new factory plus its equipment is likely to represent a 50% increase in capacity, and it will not be fully utilized initially.

The accelerator principle suggests that greater than expected growth in sales when existing plant is operating at close to capacity, generates a surge in capacity creation.

The significance of the principle is that it suggests investment spending will be erratic. For a steady growth in investment spending, there has to be a *continuous* increase in the *rate of growth* of final sales.

The existence of withdrawals suggests that such conditions are unlikely except during the upswing of the business cycle.

Investment in factories, buildings and plant and equipment has strong incomes multiplier and investment accelerator effects.

The economic cycle or business cycle is the result of the interaction of the multiplier and accelerator effect. The real world consists of businesses where risk assessment is fundamental to the investment decision. Investment spending generally only takes place when existing capacity is thought to be too low in relation to expected sales. This usually happens after a few years of continuous growth. The economic cycle is an irregular pattern of economic activity, usually around an upward trend. In the next sections we discuss the objectives that business in general will have at each stage of the cycle.

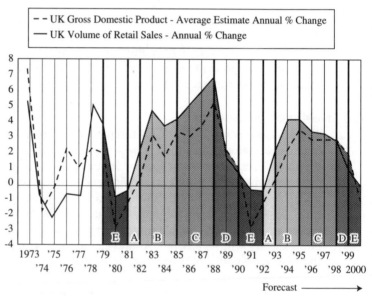

Figure 4.4   The stages of the cycle

Low point: 'the trough' (the end of stage E and the beginning of stage A)
Corporate objective: survival = cash before profit = produce strong balance sheet

All attention is on the balance sheet; the business is being managed for cash; all 'unnecessary' expenditures, e.g. advertising, training and fringe R & D cut. Production has been cut back; there is excess capacity. Sales volume static or falling. Stocks at record low levels.

Margins are under pressure because:

1 the market is increasingly price sensitive
2 lower volumes drive up average fixed cost.

A ban on recruitment, natural wastage plus selected redundancies reduces the head count – downsizing is the common description.

Strategic reviews focus on core business and disposal of non-core activities for cash.

National unemployment continues to rise, declared vacancies fall. Government borrowing rises sharply because tax receipts are below plan and Government spending is above plan (on unemployment benefit, and social security). PLC money growing very slowly.

Upswing: 'the recovery' (stage B)
Corporate objective: growth

The balance sheet is more healthy; borrowings have been cut and interest cover increased. Dividend retentions have boosted shareholders funds.

Margins have improved because of cost reduction and a significant improvement in sales volume. Production increases by more than sales (because stocks are too low). The increase in income generation suggests to many players that the worst is over; some limited recruitment. Advertising and training budgets restored. Broad money growth increases, as companies use bank finance to fund their sharply increased working capital requirement.

Growth: 'the boom' (stage C)
Corporate objective: maximize sales subject to constraints

Growth has caused a sharp increase in debtors, financed by short term borrowing and an increase in creditors.

Existing capacity is fully utilized; firms authorize increases in capital spending on new premises, plant and equipment.

Average earnings rise ahead of RPI but there is a slight drift upwards in the RPI as firms charge what the market will bear. Stock levels are low, confidence is high and increasing, leading to further recruitment. The level of unemployment falls rapidly. Sales are ahead of forecast, in some sectors there are labour and raw material bottlenecks.

The balance of payments are likely to be deteriorating as a surge of imports (of capital plant and equipment, consumer goods and raw materials) overtakes export growth.

PLC money growing rapidly, partly as the result of a spate of mergers and takeovers, partly as a result of corporate borrowing and partly as a result of increased consumer credit.

The peak and plateau (stage D)
Corporate objective: consolidate position in the market place

Sales growth below forecast, slight build in stocks. Recruitment ceases. Export markets explored. Production continues. Margins now growing as the result of price increases ahead of the RPI. Balance sheet reasonably strong: more debt finance, but gearing to meet still no more than 30%. No additional investment in capacity considered. Dividends increased. Merger and takeover activity still buoyant as cash rich firms seek to increase their market share and non cash rich firms persuade bankers that a higher level of debt is sustainable given optimistic forecasts of sales volume and margin growth. PLC money continues to grow.

The downswing (stage E)
Corporate objective: batten down to survive

Actual sales drop below planned, sudden increase in stocks. Rate of production cut below current rate of sales to reduce stocks. Balance sheet looking a bit stretched as cash generation falters. Short time working. All investment plans shelved and early redundancy scheme announced. Graduate recruitment cut. Training cut. A spate of closures caused by lack of liquidity and a change of mood from the bankers who stop lending. The balance of payments deficit narrows. The party is over, a period of balance sheet adjustment before we begin again at A.

The accelerator and multiplier principles suggest that *all booms end* and that a *constant* year on year growth in GDP is unattainable in all market economies.

Even the high growth SE Asia economies which average an 8% year on year growth rate, see swings between 4% and 10% year on year.

The following figures show the cyclical nature of the USA, Germany and Japan.

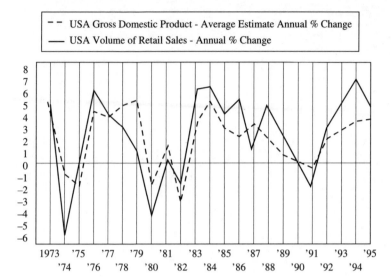

Figure 4.5 Cyclical nature of the USA

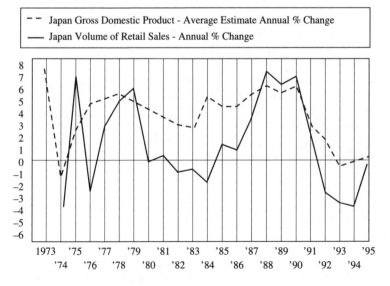

Figure 4.6 Cyclical nature of Japan

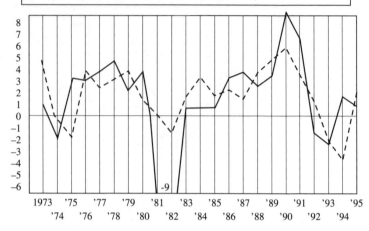

Figure 4.7   Cyclical nature of Germany

As you can see no country is the same; each experiences an economic cycle but the degree of fluctuation is different. The difference is due to differences in culture, behaviour and history.

Japan is clearly different. There appears to be no relationship between GDP and Retail Sales. This is because Japan since 1973 has an average spend of 35% of its GDP on investment. Investment spending is the largest source of demand, and produces a large positive multiplier because Japanese companies purchase investment goods from each other.

The popular explanation is that Japan has enjoyed export led growth; exports have been important (between 12% and 18% of GDP) but not as important to Japan as the UK (27% of GDP) or Germany (31% of GDP).

THE DYNAMICS OF THE SYSTEM – THE PROBLEM OF LEADS AND LAGS

Economic growth (a year on year increase in real GDP) is produced by injections exceeding withdrawals causing a multiplier effect on incomes, output and expenditure. If the multiplier effect pushes the economy close to its capacity (i.e. full employment output) then there is usually an investment surge as firms seek to increase their productive capacity to meet forecasts of ever increasing sales. This surge takes place when the economy is nearly at full capacity.

'spare capacity'	
GDP AT MARKET PRICES	TOTAL SPEND

Investment spending involves cash outlays now in anticipation of higher cash flows in the future. Investment spending adds much more to the total spend or demand side of the economy than it does to the supply side (capacity) in the short run.

This is because a new factory takes time to be completed, and no product can be supplied until completion. The lead times can vary between six months for a 'screw driver' operation and three to five years for an oil refinery. For a new combined cycle gas turbine power station the lead time is a minimum of two years.

In a market economy a surge in investment spending at near full capacity has two effects:

1   a surge in imports
2   an increase in the retail price index.

Both are the result of markets working:

		LOST TO IMPORTS
AN INFLATIONARY GAP	PRICE INCREASES	
	FULL EMPLOYMENT GDP	TOTAL SPEND

As total spend exceeds the ability of the domestic system to supply, firms and households source from abroad and domestic producers raise selling prices to *reduce* demand, with the advantage that margins, returns on capital employed and earnings per share improve.

Productive potential is an estimate of the supply side. It is measured by plotting actual output at a given level of capacity utilization.

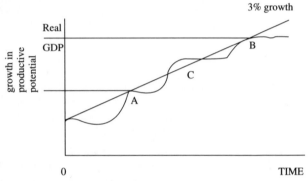

Figure 4.8 Productive potential

In Figure 4.8 at position A and B the economy is running with, say, 5% unemployment. At C it is running with 2% unemployment. At D it is running with 15% unemployment.

The 3% growth line is a trend through peaks line. At position C, the economy is growing above trend, and there is overheating – an increase in the RPI at an unpredictable rate – and a substantial deficit on the current account of the Balance of Payments.

At A and B the economy is assumed to be operating at the same rate of capacity utilization (because the % unemployed is the same), therefore the growth in output between A and B must be due to an increase in capacity not a change in the level of utilization.

Governments, like firms, just extrapolate from the past into the future using 'trend growth lines'.

If Governments can influence the level of total spending by means of fiscal and monetary policies why do they allow an economy to overheat?

The problem here is a technical and a political one.

Technically, the data on the economy is always subject to revision (i.e. the estimates of activity can be quite misleading) and it reaches the Treasury analysts some time after the economic event has happened. Then there is a time lag as the analysts work out what it all means, and then there is the lag while the Chancellor decides what steps to take (when is the election, what would these measures do for the opinion polls) and then there is the lag for the measures to take effect. Under some circumstances, because of these lags, Government could be seeking to depress activity just at the moment the need is for stimulus!

There is the analogy with a brick and an elastic band – using interest rates to change the position and direction of the economy is like pulling on the brick with an elastic band.

The first tightening has no impact; nor the second or third; but on the fourth, the brick suddenly moves forwards at a rate much faster than intended, hitting the person pulling on it hard in the back of the neck!

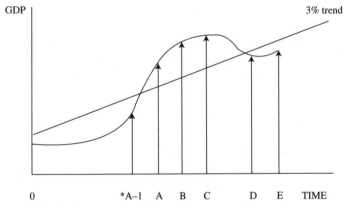

Figure 4.9   The economic picture

In Figure 4.9, at point A in time, the economic statistics available refer to A−1. They suggest that the economy is operating below trend and therefore there is spare capacity. Interest rates are lowered.

At position B in time, the figures referring to period A are available. The economy is growing more rapidly than first thought.

Government considers raising interest rates, but decides to wait until a clear picture emerges.

Interest rates are raised at C, because figures for B shows overheating.

But the economy has already turned, the higher interest rates speed the down turn; a slow down turns into a sharp recession.

At E, the figures show a deep recession (point D), Government lowers interest rates, but the economy is already recovering, thus fuelling the expansion.

THE BUSINESS CYCLE – IS IT PREDICTABLE?

The Business Cycle is a fluctuation in the rate of economic activity – a period of relatively rapid growth in GDP is followed by a period of relatively slow growth (or negative growth).

Cycle implies regularity, but the fluctuations in GDP are of varying lengths.

Taking evidence from the UK, cycles began to get longer after the 1973 oil shock. Before then, they had been about 4.5 years long (i.e. from peak to peak). The post 1973 cycle was 5.75 years and the post 1979 lasted 9.25 years.

The upsurging always ends because the economy meets its capacity limits. It is possible for a period to run above capacity but this always produces a deteriorating current account plus inflation. The last cycle showed that the UK ran above capacity to a higher level and for longer than before. This is because the balance of payments deficit was financed by capital inflows at rates of interest acceptable to the UK population.

Near the peak, profit margins get squeezed but employment and earnings continue to expand for another year before peaking and inflation a year and a half before peaking.

Once the peak is reached inflation tends to fall quite fast (the rate of increase in prices *slows* down)

Over the past 30 years, based on the United Kingdom, inflation falls by at least 6 percentage points within two years of the peak. But this is a change not a level, so if inflation was 20%, within two years it falls to 14%. The level of inflation is determined by history. It is much more powerful to get inflation down from 20% to 14% than from 8% to 2%.

The only way to do it is to depress output well below capacity.

The graph in Figure 4.10 shows the balance of payments impact of rapid growth RELATIVE to other countries.

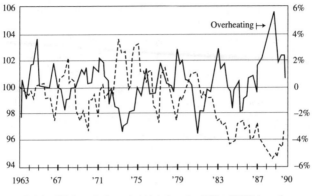

_____ Relative UK domestic demand which is the ratio of UK to OECD domestic demand deviation from long term trend (=100)

——— Non-oil current account balance of payments as a % of GDP

Figure 4.10 The relationship between relative international domestic demand and the balance of payments.
Source: Treasury Bulletin

If the UK is growing relatively faster than its trading partners, it will suck in imports from them as the figures clearly show. In 1987, the UK began to grow faster than the OECD average, and the balance of payments deficit (non-oil) hit 6% of our GDP.

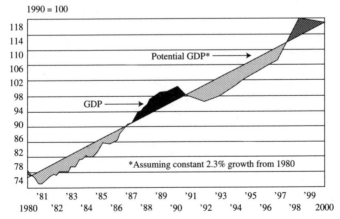

Figure 4.11 The UK output gap.
Source: CSO

CHAPTER SUMMARY

- Governments set four broad economic objectives which are mutually exclusive. They use fiscal and monetary policy to achieve them.
- The Business Cycle is the result of interaction between players in the system – in particular company investment in stocks, work in progress and new capacity.
- Destocking is a significant source of instability. It happens because of a mismatch between planned and actual sales.
- The cycle is common to all western economies; but its periodicity changes in and between countries.

5 Money and how it is manufactured

MONEY

What is money?

Anything which an individual will accept in exchange for goods and services. Once a society has moved beyond the barter stage (i.e. one sheep for one goat) then it uses various mediums of exchange. In essence there is:

Central Bank money	and	PLC money
Central Bank money is issued by the Royal Mint (coin) and the Bank of England (notes)		PLC money is created by financial institutions such as banks and finance houses

Inflation is a reduction in the value of money; because prices have gone up, a pound coin purchases less than it did before.

Consider your own position. It is likely that you only spend 10% to 20% of your income using Central Bank money. The remaining 80% to 90% of your spending is financed by PLC money.

The most common PLC money is the cheque drawn on the high street bank. The cheque is a piece of paper which people will accept in exchange for goods and services. It is not legal tender, but to most people a cheque = cash, because the cheque (PLC money) can be turned into cash (Central Bank money) at a bank, on demand.

A bank needs to manage three things:

- Security   –   a safe haven for
                           customer deposits
- Profitability   –   a satisfactory
                           return on assets
                           for shareholders
- Liquidity   –   the ability to
                           provide customers
                           with cash (Government
                           money) on demand.

Profitability and **Liquidity** tend to be inversely related.

The story on the following pages explains the essence of banking; it is supported by evidence from Lloyds Bank PLC.

THE STORY OF JONES THE LOAN

Jones the Loan is a banker who runs a stand-alone bank in a South Wales valley. Almost everyone in the community has a bank account, i.e. they have a cheque book.

At the start of this story, assume the bank has no cash or deposits, i.e., neither it nor its customers have any money. This is to keep it simple.

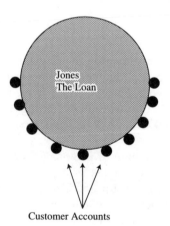

Customer Accounts

Then an outsider comes to live in the valley. Mr X decides to stay and open a bank account with Jones. He deposits £100 cash (Central Bank money) with Jones, who issues a cheque book (PLC money).

Jones, who has been running the bank for 35 years, has noticed that his customers increasingly use PLC money (cheques) rather than cash to settle transactions between themselves.

Indeed, he has worked out that on average each customer only draws 10% of their deposit in cash (Central Bank money). The rest of their deposit they spend using cheques (PLC money).

So Jones has cash of £100 (Central Bank money) but he only needs to hold £10 in the till to finance X's account. Thus leaving £90 spare.

Jones has **excess Liquidity** or more cash than he needs to support his business at the current levels.

Then the Grocer calls in to discuss the possibility of a loan. The Grocer wants to borrow £900, to pay for two unexpected bills – £400 for a new shop front (the old one fell out due to woodworm) and £500 for a replacement engine for the delivery van (the original one gave up the struggle the day before).

Jones checks that the Grocer has sufficient real assets (the freehold of the shop is valued at £40,000) to back the loan and that the Grocer is earning sufficient cash surpluses in order to pay the interest on the loan.

All looks in order and the two men have known each other since school days.

Jones grants the Grocer a loan of £900.

The Grocer leaves the bank believing that he has £900 of Government money in his current account to spend (which he hasn't, but he thinks he has). What he spends is PLC money using a PLC cheque book.

He approaches the Builder. Asks if he will take a cheque for £400. The Builder agrees. So the Grocer makes a cheque payable (PLC money) to the Builder.

The Builder banks with Jones. He pays in his cheque. The Bank clerk transfers £400 from the Grocer's account to the Builder's account (using a pencil and a rubber). The Builder makes a cheque payable to cash for £40 (PLC money in exchange for Government money).

The Bank pays out £40 in notes from the till.

The Grocer now goes to the Garage man. Makes a cheque payable for £500. The Garage man pays the cheque in.

The Bank clerk (with a pencil and a rubber) writes £500 into the Garage man's account and takes £500 from the Grocer's account.

The Garage man makes a cheque payable to cash for £50 to pay the wages.

The Bank pays out £50 in notes from the till.

In this story, Jones the Loan has created PLC money of £900, which has financed economic activity. Notice that Jones has created this 'money' from nothing; but that it is secured by assets valued at £40,000. Thus there is security, the cash provides the Liquidity and the loan gives Jones' Bank an income. Let's look at these transactions again and draw up a simple balance sheet.

Jones the Loan balance sheet

At the beginning of the story Jones has no deposits at all. Excluding bank capital, buildings etc., his balance sheet is empty.

Liabilities	Assets
Zero	Zero

Then he receives a deposit in cash of £100 from X

Liabilities	Assets
100	100

The deposit is CASH (Central Bank money) but in the name of the customer. Cash is an asset, the customer's deposit is a liability of the bank. After all, as far as X is concerned, it's his money. He can do what he likes with it, including spending it with someone who is not a customer of Jones.

When the Grocer comes in for a loan, Jones has to decide on the balance between RISK and RETURN, because Jones will be creating *PLC money of £900 out of thin air*. He also has to decide on his liquidity: the amount of the PLC money which needs to be backed by cash (Central Bank money). This decision depends on Jones' understanding of his customers, in particular their desire to hold and spend cash as opposed to PLC money (cheques).

Jones has decided that a cash ratio of 10% would give him sufficient liquidity.

He has £100 of cash. £10 has to be held to give X's account sufficient liquidity, leaving £90. This is used to provide liquidity for the creation of £900 of PLC money.

Every loan creates a deposit.

The public think that banks like Jones only lend out what they get in, i.e. every deposit creates a loan. This is not so. Banks have this unique ability to create PLC money which is spent using cheques.

They can do this because we the public choose to deposit cash (Central Bank money) with them and use their money to settle transactions by means of a cheque book.

If every loan creates a deposit, then Jones' balance sheet looks like this:

	Liabilities	Assets
X's deposit– – – –>	100	100 CASH
Grocers – – – – – –> new, created deposit	900	900 LOAN TO GROCER
	1000	1000

What are the limits to growth of Jones' balance sheet?

1   The net amount of cash (Central Bank money) Jones needs to hold to provide sufficient liquidity.
2   The amount of cash customers are willing to deposit with him.
3   The willingness of people like the Grocer to borrow.
4   The risk assessment by Jones, i.e. the ability of the Grocer to pay the interest and the capital.

In the real world there is a fifth limit called the capital asset ratio of 8%. More on this later in Chapter 6.

Measuring the money supply

M0   is the narrow definition of money. It measures notes and coin issued by the Central Bank. Also included in M0 is Bankers' Operational Deposits at the Bank of England -more on these later.

M4 is MO plus bank deposits and Building Society deposits. This is known as Broad money.

In the Jones example, MO = £100 and M4 is £1000 (i.e. £100 = MO plus £900 non cash deposits)

The main component of broad money is PLC money created by the banks

In Figure 5.1 you will see a summary of Lloyds Bank's Balance Sheet.

You will notice that in 1987, Lloyds operated very like Jones' Bank. Lloyds held 11.8% of deposits in cash (Central Bank money or its equivalent).

Its loans (Advances = PLC money) outstanding were £25.7 Billion. The interest payable on this is Lloyds' main source of income.

In 1987, there was little scope for Lloyds to create more PLC money if it viewed the 11.8% cash ratio as prudent. That is allowing sufficient liquidity. Lloyds will have agreed with the Bank of England a liquidity ratio, which is unpublished. More PLC money could be created by Lloyds **if** more of its customers used less cash (and deposited it with Lloyds); and there was an increase in the number of willing borrowers which had a 'credit risk' acceptable to Lloyds.

By 1988, Lloyds had expanded its balance sheet. Over the year it had created 17% more PLC money (advances went from £25.7Bn to £31Bn.) but it had increased its cash by 27%. So in 1988 Lloyds had not expanded its lending by as much as it could, given its cash base.

The reasons for this are related to the bank's corporate strategy, which is to do things which will increase the return on capital employed.

This can be delivered in a number of ways; either Lloyds could increase the volume of lending or it could increase the quality of lending, which means a higher margin. Lloyds have chosen to expand their lending only when it is profitable to do so, commensurate with an agreed level of risk. A loan which goes wrong, i.e., the lender fails to pay interest due on the day and is unable to pay off the capital, reduces the return on capital employed.

Skipping ahead to 1989 and 1990 you can see that Lloyds in 1990 *stopped creating PLC money*, simply because the recession

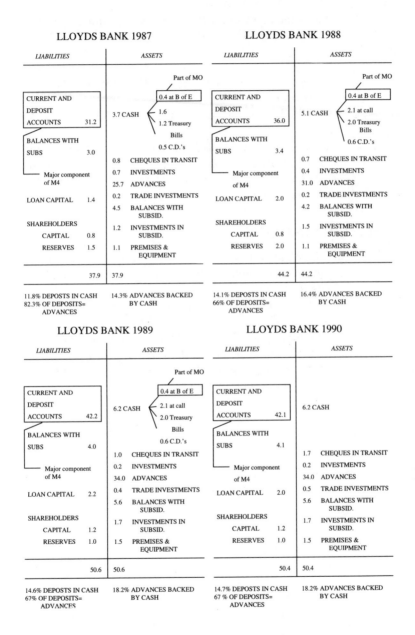

Figure 5.1 Summary of Lloyds Bank's balance sheets.

reduced the demand for PLC money and simultaneously raised the risk of lending, as asset prices (property and land) stopped rising or fell.

WHEN BANKS INCREASE THEIR LENDING, PLC MONEY IS CREATED.
WHEN BANKS REDUCE THEIR LENDING, PLC MONEY IS DESTROYED.
In the UK 75% of all bank lending is secured against land or property, and as we shall see later in the book, land and property prices have an impact on banks' lending decisions and therefore the money supply.

CHAPTER SUMMARY

- There are two types of money; notes and coin manufactured by the Central Bank and bank deposits manufactured by the banking system.
- Banks can create deposits because their customers use cheques and credit transfers to settle their debts. Banks can create deposits up to 12.5 times their capital base. The extent to which they do this depends on their assessment of risk and the customers' willingness to take on debt. The rate of interest and asset prices are important determinants.

6 The government and the money supply

THE GOVERNMENT AND THE MONEY SUPPLY

The Government is concerned to meet its objectives. Monetary policy is one of the means. Fiscal policy is the other.

Monetary policy means varying the price and availability of money, and influencing the exchange rate to have an impact on the value of money (the inflation rate) and the volume of economic activity (GDP in real terms).

Fiscal policy means altering the structure and level of taxation in relation to the structure and level of Government spending to have an impact on the value of money and the volume of economic activity. If Government has a budget surplus or deficit, both have implications for monetary policy.

In short, fiscal policy cannot be conducted without its impact on the money supply being fully assessed.

The banks do not just lend to the public, they lend to the Government. Lending to the public is discretionary but lending to the Government is automatic.

The way in which all this works is quite complex, but there are basic principles which, if kept in mind, make it clear.

Principle No. I

Banks are always managing their affairs to balance

SECURITY   LIQUIDITY   and   PROFITABILITY

Principle No. II

Banks are PLCs owned by shareholders. They are *not* interested in Government monetary policy unless it has an impact on their ability to create shareholder value and provide security for their customers.

Principle No. III

The rate of interest is the price of money. It is determined by supply and demand. The rate of interest changes if supply changes and demand is held constant, or if demand changes and supply is held constant, or some combination of the two.

Principle No. IV

Money and its price affects almost all of the population. It is therefore a political issue. People generally prefer Governments which lower interest rates to Governments which raise them. If interest rates are rising in the year before an election, Governments tend to be thrown out. But if interest rates are falling, they tend to be re-elected.

MONETARY POLICY IN PRACTICE IN THE UNITED KINGDOM

The conduct of monetary policy is one of the Bank of England's key responsibilities. The Bank acts as adviser to the Government in this respect, and carries out agreed decisions in the markets. Activity in the money market by the Bank is reported as action taken by 'the authorities'.

Monetary policy is concerned with varying the price and availability of money in the economy. The principal objective is to maintain the value of money – or to put it another way – to, in principle, ensure that the rate of inflation is zero. If monetary conditions are too loose – for example, if interest rates are not high enough – then there is excessive creation of PLC money which is spent and a weaker exchange rate against other currencies, leading to upward pressure on costs and prices. A tight monetary policy, on the other hand, involving high real interest rates (i.e., the interest rate is higher than the inflation rate) will tend to slow the growth of spending, the creation of PLC money and prices, but may also slow output and investment, usually leading to increased unemployment.

Proper control over monetary conditions is thought to be necessary to achieve sustainable economic growth. Since 1980, the underlying policy framework has been set out each year in the Medium-Term Financial Strategy, published by the Treasury at the time of the Budget. The objective, as expressed in successive versions of the MTFS, has been to ensure that monetary and fiscal policy complement one another to defeat inflation.

In the early 1980s the MTFS laid great emphasis on achieving targets for the growth of broad money; since the mid-1980s more emphasis has been given to a range of indicators of spending and inflationary pressure. The only targeted monetary aggregate was the narrow measure, MO, which was set at 0% – 4%.

From October 1990 and September 1992, when the UK was in the Exchange Rate Mechanism, the overriding objective was to maintain the value of sterling within its permitted bands of fluctuation, but a target for MO was still set.

Techniques
Operations in the domestic money market
In a modern market economy, the main instrument of monetary policy is the short-term interest rate which is the rate at which banks lend to each other for 3 months. As the ultimate provider of liquidity to the banking system, the central bank can determine the cost to the banks of liquidity and thus influence the pattern of short-term rates throughout the economy. Here, such influence is exercised through the Bank of England's daily operations in the money markets, conducted mainly with the discount houses who accept secured deposits from the banks and hold portfolios of sterling money market instruments. They have a direct dealing relationship with the Bank, and borrowing facilities at the Bank. Throughout most of the 1980s banks deposited 6% of their stock of bills with the discount houses. This was known as 'club money' and was a form of subscription. In the early 1990s, the banks have ignored this rule and sharply reduced their club money.

The Bank acts as banker to the Government and to the commercial banks. Each working day the banks clear cheques drawn on their customers accounts.

Each bank has an account with the Bank of England. At the end of each day, the banks settle their cash positions, using their account at the Bank. They are expected to hold 0.4% of their liabilities in cash in their Bank of England account. They are not expected to fall below this level. Also any transactions between the Government and the non-bank public are cleared through the same account. For example, if you make a cheque payable to the Inland Revenue for £100 when the cheque is cleared your bank's cash falls by £100 and the Bank's cash increases by £100.

The Bank monitors very closely the movement of funds between the Government and the private sector. If, on any particular day, more funds move from the banks' accounts to the Government's accounts than vice versa (for example, because the banks' customers are paying their taxes or purchasing new issues of gilts) then the money market will be short of funds. If the balance of flows goes the other way (perhaps because the Government is paying its bills), then the market will be in surplus.

Generally, the operation of the Government accounts, including the weekly issue of Treasury Bills to the market, results in the money market starting each day with a prospective shortage.

During the course of the day the Bank, through its purchases of bills from the discount houses and if necessary by lending direct to the houses, will relieve the shortage.

On a day-to-day basis, the Bank's objective is to avoid the sharp fluctuations in interest rates that would arise if market shortages or surpluses were not relieved. But the Bank's transactions with and loans to the market are at rates of its own choosing, and if the authorities (the Treasury after consulting the Bank) decide that a change in short-term interest rates is appropriate then the Bank will change the rates at which it relieves the day's shortage or surplus; such a change will normally be quickly reflected in the base rates set by the banks for lending to their own customers. Thus a change in monetary policy becomes operational.

The Bank may sometimes signal a change in rates by publicly announcing the rate at which it will lend to the discount houses that day (normally the rates on such loans are not disclosed). Such an announcement may also be used to curb expectations of a change in rates. In the past, before the present arrangements were introduced in 1981, the Bank continuously posted a Bank Rate or Minimum Lending Rate, but such an official rate is now declared only in exceptional circumstances, as on September 16th 1992, when the UK made a final attempt to stay within the ERM bands.

On that day a change in the Bank's direct lending policy became necessary.

On September 16th 1992, the Bank purchased billions of pounds to maintain its value around Dm2.95: This produced a shortage of sterling assets in the market which the discount houses were unable to relieve (their holdings of cash were insufficient). To avoid higher short-term interest rates, the Bank announced that for a month banks and building societies could borrow cash directly from the Bank without going through the discount houses, backed by their holding of gilt-edged. This scheme has been extended and from 1994 onwards, big cash shortages can be met from direct borrowing. The discount houses are losing their unique status as the route to the Bank for the clearing banks. However they are attracting more business from large corporates which these days place their cash direct, in the market, instead of via their bank, a process known as disintermediation. The rate at which the Bank offsets cash shortages with the discount houses is still expected to provide the signal to the market for the level and direction of interest rates.

THE EFFECTS OF CHANGES IN INTEREST RATES

A change in interest rates will affect the economy through a number of routes. First, a change in the cost of borrowing will affect spending decisions. Interest rates affect the relative attraction of spending today as against spending later, in that a rise in rates will make saving more attractive and borrowing less so, and this will tend to reduce present spending, both on consumption and on investment.

Second, a change in rates affects the discretionary incomes of borrowers. People on average in 1990 devoted 14% of their income to servicing debt, and since the mid-1980s the personal sector as a whole has had more variable-rate debts than assets; a rise or fall in interest rates therefore has quite a significant impact on their outgoings and their discretionary income. Companies, similarly, are net debtors, and their exposure to interest rate changes has also increased in the past seven years. An increase in interest rates reduces earnings per share and profits available for reinvestment or distribution to shareholders.

Third, a change in interest rates affects the value of certain assets, notably housing and stocks and shares. In the UK, a change in rates can have a particularly visible effect on house prices, and that in turn will influence people's willingness to borrow and spend money.

All of these influences will determine the level of spending and there will be further multiplier effects on spending from rising or falling company profits and employment. For example, lower spending and activity are likely to have an effect on prices, partly because of the pressure on company profits and partly because wage pressures will be less.

A particular influence on prices comes through the exchange rate. For example, a rise in domestic interest rates relative to those overseas will tend to cause the exchange rates to rise, and that will reduce import prices (which represent 27% of GDP at market prices) increase competitive pressures and supplement the downward pressure on inflation arising from weakened demand. Historically, a 10% change in the exchange rate, moves the retail price index 3% within two years; revaluation reduces retail prices, a devaluation increases them.

Operations in the foreign exchange market

In addition to their direct effects on the domestic economy, movements in interest rates influence the value of sterling in terms of other currencies.

If interest rates on sterling deposits rise in relation to rates on other currencies, then (other things remaining equal) money will flow into sterling and sterling's exchange rate will rise. The exchange rate will also, of course, reflect market expectations about economic, financial and political developments here and abroad, so that a rise in interest rates may not always result in a higher exchange rate.

The Bank can also attempt to influence the exchange rate through direct market intervention, using for the purpose the country's foreign exchange reserves. (These are owned by the Treasury and held in a fund called the Exchange Equalization Account which is managed by the Bank on the Treasury's behalf.) When sterling is weak, the Bank can enter the market to buy sterling for foreign currencies; this may help to limit sterling's decline.

Alternatively, if sterling is strong the Bank can sell sterling for foreign currencies.

When the UK was a member of the European Exchange Rate Mechanism it was obliged to keep the exchange rate of sterling within pre-set limits relative to the other currencies in the mechanism. Until August 2nd 1993, most ERM members kept their currencies within margins of approximately 2.25% either side of their agreed central rates, but the UK, along with Spain, had margins of approximately 6%. Thus, sterling's permitted variation against the Deutsche Mark were 6% either side of the central rate of DM2.95 – in effect, a range of DM2.78–3.13. Similar ranges were established for each of the other ERM currencies, and if sterling moved to its limit against any of them, the authorities in both countries were obliged to intervene or change interest rates to prevent the limit being breached. Since August 2nd 1993, the margin is 15% either side of the agreed central rate, for the remaining members of the ERM but not the UK.

At the bilateral margins, the Bank's obligation to buy or sell sterling for foreign exchange was unlimited. But the Bank could also intervene before the official intervention points were reached, in order to smooth erratic movements or to signal the authorities' intentions.

Operations in the government securities market

As well as acting as the Government's banker, the Bank acts for the Government in raising loans in the markets. The weekly tender for Treasury bills – Government IOUs issued at a discount for payment usually in three or six months – is mainly directed at managing the liquidity of the money market. The Government's borrowing requirement – The Public Sector Borrowing Requirement – is funded mainly by long-term borrowing in the market for government securities, or gilt-edged stock. This market is centred on a group of specialized market makers who have direct dealing arrangements with the Bank, and who ensure that the market is deep and liquid – gilts are widely held and traded by domestic and foreign institutions and by private investors.

The general principle is that any PSBR (together with the sterling used in intervention to acquire foreign exchange) should be funded in full by sales of Government debt to the domestic private sector other than the banks and the building societies, and to overseas investors. Financing the deficit through the banking system could add to monetary growth in a potentially inflationary way. This principle was modified in the 1993 March budget, to allow greater monetary growth.

During the early 1980s the Government deliberately sold more debt outside the banking system than was needed to finance its deficit: this overfunding reduced bank deposits and thus the growth of broad money, which was at the time subject to an annual target.

It also drained money market liquidity, and to prevent unintended increases in interest rates this had to be returned by the Bank of England's purchase of short-term commercial bills from the banking system in its daily operations. Such a pattern of operations meant that the authorities were borrowing at higher long-term interest rates relative to short-term rates.

Overfunding was ended in 1985, and in the following year broad money targets were formally abandoned. Since then, the general objective has been a full fund of the public sector's transactions, including the sterling counterpart of foreign exchange market intervention. When the public sector moved into surplus in 1988, the full-fund rule implied buying back gilts from the private sector (other than from banks and building societies) in order to continue to neutralize the effects of public sector transactions on private sector liquidity. This is what the authorities did, mainly by operations in the market but also by a series of reverse auctions. The recent return to a PSBR has meant a return to a programme of gilts issues and concern for excessively low broad money growth has led to underfunding.

THE DEVELOPMENT OF POLICY

The past twenty years have seen monetary policy occupy a steadily more prominent role in economic management in the UK. For much of the 1950s and 1960s, monetary conditions were seen essentially as a by-product of other policies – which included from time to time a number of direct controls on, for example, wages, dividends and prices.

Monetary policy, too, depended on direct controls – for example, there was much reliance on restrictions on consumer credit and on bank lending in general. Mortgages were effectively rationed throughout the period. This was also of course a period in which the UK had restrictive exchange controls and adhered to the Bretton Woods regime of generally fixed exchange rates against the dollar. The collapse of Bretton Woods in 1971–72, and the world-wide inflationary conditions of the 1970s, led to much closer attention to monetary policy in all countries.

In 1971 the UK moved to a more market-related monetary environment under a policy known as Competition and Credit Control. The former quantitative ceilings on bank lending were lifted, and interest rates were allowed a larger role in the allocation of credit. This coincided with a period of fiscal expansion and rapid growth of demand in the economy, and monetary expansion was also rapid as banks increased their lending and competed in the inter-bank market for deposits.

A form of quantitative control was reintroduced in 1973 in the form of the Supplementary Special Deposit Scheme, also known as the Corset. It imposed penalties on banks whose interest-bearing deposits grew faster than a pre-set limit. The Corset was not abolished until 1980.

From the mid-1970s there was increased academic and practical interest in the concept of monetary targeting, and in 1976 the government adopted a target for broad money. The MTFS, first introduced in 1980, placed considerable emphasis on monetary targets; initially broad money (M3), later a range of aggregates, and then (from 1987) M0 alone. The point of such intermediate targets ('intermediate' in the sense that the real objective was to reduce inflation, and the monetary target was intended to provide a tangible link between the chosen policy instrument of interest rates and the ultimate objective) was that they could be seen to provide a framework and benchmark for policy. But they could do so only for so long as they would themselves respond to the policy instruments and demonstrate a stable and predictable link with the ultimate objective.

In practice, the link was never very clear cut and became increasingly less so as financial innovation and structural change in the markets affected the behaviour of the monetary aggregates and undermined previous assumptions about the relationship between money, economic growth and inflation.

With the end of broad money targets after 1986, the possibilities of exchange rate targets began to attract more attention, particularly in the context of possible entry to the Exchange Rate Mechanism.

The exchange rate became one of the indicators of which the authorities 'took account' in deciding monetary policy and for a period an informal attempt was made to constrain sterling within a narrow trading range just below DM3=£1. That episode coincided with a period of upward pressure on sterling and of excessive domestic demand; the low interest rates necessary to maintain the informal trading range were insufficient to head off the developing inflationary pressures and the policy was abandoned. But in October 1990, when sterling formally entered the Exchange Rate Mechanism, this formalized the role of exchange rate targeting in UK monetary policy. The ERM provided a binding external constraint on domestic policy, since interest rates now needed to be consistent with sterling's ERM priorities. The UK left the ERM when this constraint was perceived by the markets to be unsustainable.

SOME ALTERNATIVE APPROACHES

Over the years a range of possible alternative techniques of monetary control has been suggested. Some have been rejected; others have influenced policy formulation without becoming, as their original champions would have liked, the sole basis for policy. For example, monetary targets were at one stage thought by some capable of carrying the whole weight of policy formulation. In practice, the monetary aggregates have not proved reliable enough to play this role, although they are seen as important indicators. Some other suggestions have included the following:

Monetary base control

The money supply is given by the deposit liabilities of the banking system, and it is tempting to suppose that if there were a stable relationship between some or all of these liabilities and the 'base money' requirements of the banking system (that is, the system's holdings of balances at the Bank of England and notes and coin), then the authorities might be able to control the money supply by controlling the *amount* of base money. However, quite apart from the difficulties associated with the variability of demand for base money (and the likelihood that the relationship will change as banks adapted to the control), such a system could have unwelcome effects on liquidity and on the volatility of interest rates in the short-term markets, without necessarily yielding any more practical or effective means of monetary control than current methods provide.

Direct controls on lending

Direct controls on credit are often suggested as an alternative to reliance on interest rates. However, as was demonstrated in the 1950s and 1960s they introduce rigidities and reduce competition in the financial system. In today's world of deregulated and sophisticated international financial markets, borrowers and lenders would almost certainly be successful in avoiding such controls. With the increased mobility of capital and the dismantling of exchange controls, national monetary authorities can no longer hope to isolate their financial markets from international influences.

Not surprisingly under these circumstances, most monetary authorities world-wide which used to rely on credit controls have either ended them or are in the process of doing so. However, were credit thought to be expanding too rapidly, then credit controls could be used as an emergency brake.

Reserve ratios

In some countries, banks are required to place a proportion of their liabilities as deposits, often non-interest bearing, with the central bank. These requirements can be used to create the liquidity shortages through which the central bank influences interest rates. When they are non-interest bearing, they also affect the size of the margin above money market rates that the banks need to charge on loans to their customers. To the borrowers, the effect is indistinguishable from that of a higher general level of interest rates. It is sometimes argued that setting such ratios, and the ability to vary them, would constitute a useful measure of monetary control in the UK. However, by adjusting the Treasury bill issue, the Bank has no difficulty under the present arrangements in creating the shortages of liquidity necessary for its money market operation; and consequently it has suggested that it requires no additional devices for varying interest rates by for example operating directly on banks' profit margins.

To the extent that reserve ratios serve as a tax on bank inter-mediation of funds, they make the country's banking system less efficient and competitive. The Bank does have the facility to call for special deposits; these would be interest-bearing, but no call has been made since 1979. There is also a requirement on the banks to place a small proportion – currently 0.4% – of their liabilities with the Bank of England on a non-interest bearing basis. This has no monetary policy purpose – the intention is simply to secure the income and resources of the Bank, and the ratio is reviewed from time to time in the light of that requirement alone. Indeed, it was reduced from 0.4% to 0.5% in January 1991 because the Abbey National became a bank and deposited money in this account.

Capital ratios

From 1st January 1993 all international banks (i.e., any bank that operates outside the domestic market) are required by the Bank of International Settlements to hold at least 8% of their assets in the form of shareholders funds such as retained profits, long term loans and share premium account.

This is not a liquidity requirement (which will vary between countries and is determined by the relevant central bank) but a capital requirement. It means that banks are not able to grow their assets by more than 12.5 times their capital.

So a bank with £8 Billion capital cannot increase its balance sheet by more than £100 Billion.

To increase their balance sheets banks would have to obtain more capital by way of equity issue, retained profits, or long term loans.

Profitability is more important than ever to allow sufficient retentions to build the business.

The credit crunch

When banks have advances which are non-performing, i.e., the stream of income from them is sporadic or non-existent or they are secured against assets which are losing value, a prudent bank makes provisions. This is a charge against the Profit and Loss account. The higher the provision, the lower the profit available for retention (to increase the capital base) or distribution to share-holders.

The effect is to reduce a bank's ability to create more advances even if there are willing borrowers.

In July 1992 some observers suggested that in the UK, USA and Japan a credit crunch existed; all three economies were experiencing very low rates of increase in broad money. By 1995, all except Japan had recovered and bank lending was growing again.

MONETARY INSTRUMENTS

What is a Treasury Bill?

It is a short term security issued for 91 days. The yield (or interest rate) is determined by the purchase price in relation to the nominal value.

Nominal Values are   £5,000
                            £10,000 upwards to £1,000,000.

For example, assume that London money market rates are currently 12.5%. Discount houses can obtain call money at this rate. They would want to earn at least 12.5% on their holding of Treasury Bills.

They calculate a bid price of £9,676 for a £10,000 nominal Bill in the following manner.

91 day TB nominal	£10,000
offer price	£9,676
capital gain =	£324 in 91 days
simple interest	£324 × 4 = £1296
	which is 12.96%
(compound interest rate is 13%)	
if the offer price increases to £9,800	
capital gain is	£200 in 91 days
simple interest	£200 × 4 = £800
	which is 8%

The discount houses purchase and sell Treasury Bills on a discount per annum basis using the following formula:

$$\text{Discount} = \text{principal} \times \frac{\text{rate}}{100} \times \frac{\text{days}}{365}$$

$$\text{£}323.11 = 10,000 \times \frac{12.96}{100} \times \frac{91}{365}$$

How to spot signs of a change in monetary policy

WHAT TO WATCH 1

The Bank of England's operations with the Market

Every working day a vast number of transactions take place involving payments between the Bank of England and the banking system. The effect of this is that the Clearing and other banks find themselves either with a surplus or a deficit of funds.

When money is in surplus, usually because of official payments on behalf of Government Departments, the Bank will normally 'mop up' the excess by selling Treasury Bills to the market or the banks, or both. These Treasury Bills will normally be of short duration, probably maturing on the day when money is next expected to be short.

When the net flow is in the opposite direction, the banks, to restore their own cash positions, will call money from the discount houses who will be left with a shortage.

The Bank of England has various methods of relieving a shortage in the Market.

1   **Outright purchases**
The Bank of England buys Treasury Bills, Corporation Bills, and Eligible Bank Bills offered by the discount houses. Maturity dates are set by the Bank and are expressed in terms of a band. This can take place in the morning and afternoon.

2   **Repurchase agreements**
The Bank of England buys Treasury Bills, Corporation Bills and Eligible Bank Bills offered by the Discount Market, with an agreement that the houses repurchase the bills on a set date. This can take place in the morning and afternoon.

3 **Lending**
The Bank of England invites the Discount Market to borrow at 2.30 p.m. This is usually on the basis of overnight or seven days.

The Bank of England's open market operations are disclosed together with the range of dates dealt in and the maturities of the bills purchased or sold. The maturities are expressed in terms of bands which are as follows:

Band 1 = Up to 14 Days
Band 2 = 15–33 Days
Band 3 = 34–63 Days
Band 4 = 64–91 Days

4 **Direct Lending to large banks and building societies**
These institutions are allowed to borrow direct from the Bank, secured against their holding of gilt edged securities.

Market rates

The following are important:

1 **Base rate**
which is the rate prevailing between the banking system and its customers.

2 **Interbank rate**
which is the rate between banks in the banking system.

3 **'Discount rate'**
which is the rate between the Discount Market and the Bank of England.

Interbank and Base Rates are readily available. The 'Discount Rates' to watch are:

Band 1 (the Bank of England's up to 14 day intervention rate)
Band 2 (the Bank of England's 15–33 day intervention rate) and for the 3 months period, the true yield equivalent of the average discount rate of the previous Friday's Treasury Bill tender.

WHAT TO WATCH 2

Financial Press

Attention should be paid to the comparison of money market rates published in the financial press. Clues can often be obtained as to the likely movements of interest rates by understanding the significance of the terms used by newspapers in their daily money market report.

At 9.45 a.m. the Bank of England publishes a forecast for the day with a breakdown of the factors contributing to a surplus (+) or a deficit (−). At approximately 12.40p.m. and 2.40p.m. the Bank publishes details (if any) of its dealings with the discount houses. This information is also made available to the various press agencies – the FT uses this information to produce its money market report.

Every week day the Financial Times used to publish a narrative under the heading 'Money Markets'.

This describes the operation of the Bank of England in the money market on the previous day. The extracts reproduced below were published on 24th July 1991, with the title 'Money Markets – Rates Hold Steady'.

Three month sterling inter-bank lending was $11\frac{1}{16}$–11%. Lending for 12 months was at a slightly lower interest rate.

This suggests that the lenders expect short term interest rates to fall over the next twelve months. Liffe is the London International Financial Futures Exchange where traders guess the future course of interest rates and back their hunches by accepting packets of money at different interest rates and agreeing to supply packets at different interest rates.

The Bank of England did not absorb a fairly large shortage of Liquidity.

This means that the discount houses were short of cash which the Bank chose not to supply; so they had to borrow (at higher rates) from banks and large companies, like ICI and BP, which trade in the market directly.

The shortage was forecast to be £850m revised to £800m at noon and back to £850m in the afternoon. The Bank provided help of £534m.

This means that it supplied £534m of cash in return for Bank Bills and Treasury Bills. The narrative explains how the help was given.

Band I   Bills maturing within 14 days

Band II   Bills maturing 15–33 days

Bank Bills are issued by banks, Treasury Bills by the Bank of England, both are offered for sale for cash. Both can be 'discounted' for cash at any time, with the discount houses.

The Bank can determine the level of short term interest rates by means of this 'open market' operation.

Bills maturing in official hands, repayment of late assistance and a take up of Treasury Bills drained £170m.

This means that on previous days the Bank has taken in Bills for cash, but expects them to be repurchased (refinanced) on maturity. Late assistance is direct lending to the discount houses.

A take up of treasury bills means that treasury bills offered on the previous Thursday are being 'drip fed' into the market for cash.

Exchequer Transactions absorbing £720m.

Means that people are paying their taxes. All transactions between the public and the Government are 'cash'.

These outweighed a fall in the note circulation adding 50m to liquidity.

The note circulation is cash in the system. On a Friday people draw out cash for the weekend. The cash moves from the clearing banks to the public. But when the cash is spent over the weekend it finds its way back into the banks who are able to place it on the market overnight or for longer. A fall in the note circulation means the public are demanding less cash. A rise in the note circulation means they are demanding more cash. In summary, more cash in the public's pocket means less in the money market.

Since 1994 the FT has no longer given the detail as described. Instead they have broadened their coverage of other financial markets and reduced the detail to a single paragraph.

What causes changes in the rate of interest?

There is no single rate of interest in the economy. For example the interest rate on credit cards can be 35%, whilst on overdrafts 18%, on mortgage 14%, and interbank 11%. The different rates represent supply and demand, and the degree of risk and competition in each market.

The short-term interest rate

This is the rate which rules in the London Money Market on a minute by minute basis. It is determined by the way in which the Bank operates in the market to relieve a shortage of liquidity (cash) or mop up excess liquidity (cash).

The long-term interest rate

This is the rate of interest on long-dated gilt edged securities. It is determined by supply and demand and, in particular, inflationary expectations.

What is a gilt (or a bond)?

A gilt is a bond issued by the Bank of England on behalf of the Treasury which pays either a fixed rate of interest or a rate linked to inflation.

Some will definitely be redeemed for a fixed sum on a fixed date; others (undated stock) will never be repaid; the repayment value of index-linked gilts increases in line with inflation.

However, if market interest rates rise to 12 per cent, then investors may well be tempted to sell their gilts and put their money elsewhere. The price of gilts will fall, but an investor who buys the gilt for, say, £90 will still receive a coupon of £10. He will also, if he holds the gilt to maturity, make a profit of £10.

The relationship between the return on a gilt and its price is called the yield. In the above case, with a coupon of £10 and a market price of £90, the interest-only, or running yield, as it is known, is 11.1 per cent.

However, markets also take account of the fact that the gilt will eventually be redeemed. If the gilt is to be repaid in 12 months' time, the investor will earn a coupon of £10 and a capital gain of £10: £20 in total for an outlay of £90. This return is expressed as the gross yield to redemption, which in this case would be 22.2 per cent.

Yields have an inverse relationship with bond prices. If yields fall, prices rise and vice versa. Successful investment in gilts partly depends on timing. Buying just before interest rates fall will result in a capital gain; buying just before they rise will result in a loss.

Unfortunately, it is very difficult to predict the future course of interest rates. Even if you could, it is not possible to be certain exactly by how much a fall in interest rates will result in a rise in bond prices. Many factors come into play. (These arguments apply to fixed rate rather than index-linked issues).

The structure of interest rates in the UK economy

Borrowers pay different interest rates depending on the period of the loan. Gilts have different yields depending on their redemption dates. The line which plots yields from the very short term (one week) to the very long term (25 years) is known as the yield curve.

In theory, the yield curve should normally slope upward, that is, long-term rates should be higher than short-term. This is because lenders would normally be expected to demand a higher price for committing their money for longer.

However, the yield curve can be inverted – that is, short-term rates are higher than long-term rates. If rates are 14 per cent, while long-dated gilts are yielding around 10 per cent, this indicates that investors believe short-term interest rates are unusually high and that they will eventually fall.

The rate of inflation

Another factor which affects the yield on gilts is inflation. Normally, investors will demand a return that more than compensates them for the expected increase in the Retail Price Index. If the current rate of inflation is 9.3 per cent and the yield on long gilts is around 10 per cent – the difference, known as the real yield, is 0.7 per cent.

However, the quoted rate of inflation only refers to last year's increase in prices. The investor who buys a gilt now is worried about future inflation.

The Government's finances

As with any other commodity, the price of a gilt depends on supply and demand. When the Government is reducing its borrowing because it has been spending less than its income from taxation

– in short, it has maintained a budget surplus –the shortfall in gilt supply keeps prices higher and yields lower than might otherwise occur.

However, recession which reduces tax revenues and increases social services spending, pushes the budget into deficit. The Government has to borrow and is, therefore, issuing gilts. The more it issues, the more it will approach the point when investors are sated with gilts and will demand a higher yield for buying more; in other words, prices will fall.

The expected strength of the pound

UK investors are not the only people who are interested in buying gilts. There are many overseas holders of UK Government bonds and they face a risk if sterling falls. If they think sterling is likely to fall they will sell gilts, pushing prices down; and if they think that sterling is about to rise, they will buy gilts, pushing prices up.

All these factors can act together. When inflation is high, the pound may decline and interest rates will be increased to support the pound and control price rises. Such a combination would be bad for gilts.

The arguments in favour of gilts are simply if inflation is on the way down; interest rates are expected to fall, as the government tries to pull the economy out of recession.

Where can I buy gilts?

The National Savings Stock Register

The cheapest way to invest, and probably the most convenient. You can pick up the forms in a post office and post your application using a pre-paid envelope. You can choose between spending a certain amount, or buying gilts of a certain face value and leaving officials to fill in your cheque. Sales can be done the same way.

Low commissions are the biggest advantage. You only need to pay £1 on the first £250 you spend on gilts of a certain face value, leaving officials to fill in your cheque. Sales can be done the same way.

The transaction, however, is clumsy. The Bonds and Stock Office try to complete deals received in the first post by the end of that working day. Therefore, if you post your application early on Monday, you will buy at Tuesday's closing price – a lot can happen in two days' trading. Postal delays could send your calculations further away.

Post offices do not offer an investment advice service, so you will need to do your homework.

High street banks

More convenient than the post office, as transactions can usually be handled on the spot and advice is available (provided you fill out the relevant forms), but commissions are higher. For example, NatWest charges 1.0% and Lloyds 0.5% commission, both with a minimum of £25.

Stockbrokers

Advisable if you have your own privately managed portfolio. Commissions are negotiable, but generally start at about 1.15 % for the first £5,000 invested, decreasing in bands after that.

The advantages of advice on strategy, and the ability to buy at exactly the price you want, will be valuable for those with large sums to invest.

Unit Trusts

A convenient way to invest, which provides a broad spread. Gilts and bonds trusts can be bought in the same way as equity funds. Sixty are now on offer, according to the Unit Trust Association. Commissions shave about 1% from net income.

Do I have to buy a minimum or maximum amount?

No.

If you buy via the stock register there is a limit of spending £10,000 on any one stock on a particular day, but you can spend more than this if you spread it among different stocks. There is no maximum limit on unit trusts.

Minimum commission charges should deter you from investing in gilts via stockbrokers unless you are spending bigger sums – four figures at the very least. There is no minimum charge.

What are the different gilts on the market?

Government bonds present different investment propositions, depending on the coupon and the length of time to expiry. The best one for you depends on your own circumstances.

Sub-divisions, as listed in the FT, are as follows:-

9 short-dated – to be redeemed in the next five years.
9 medium-dated – redemption between five and 10 years
9 long-dated – redeemable after more than 15 years
9 undated – no latest date given for redemption.

As a rule, the shorter the period left before redemption, the smaller the price fluctuations because investors know the gilt will shortly be redeemed in full. Undated stock is more at the mercy of interest rates.

Higher coupons tend to lead to steadier prices and yields.

How will I be paid my interest?

You can have interest paid into a current account. Otherwise, it comes in the post, in the form of a crossed warrant.

How do I work out the price I will need to pay?

Prices are quoted in units of £$\frac{1}{33}$ (just over 3p) for shorts and of £$\frac{1}{16}$ (just over 6p) for all others, and can be read daily in the FT under 'British Funds' in the London Share Service.

Bear in mind that the price quoted in the FT is the mid-point between the buying and selling prices – you will have to pay more than this price to buy, and receive less if selling.

However, if you buy the stock cum dividend – when you are still eligible for the next dividend – you must pay more than the quoted price because it does not include interest which has accrued since the last dividend.

Similarly, if you buy ex-dividend – five weeks before dividends are payable – you pay less and wait longer for your first dividend.

To work out accrued interest in pence, take the number of weeks since the last dividend (or until the next one if your gilts are ex-dividend), multiply it by the coupon, and double it. Add this to cum dividend prices, and subtract it from ex-dividend for the approximate price you will have to pay.

How much tax do I need to pay?

Gilts investments are exempt from Capital Gains Tax. However, although payments of interest are made gross, you are liable to pay income tax at your highest rate. This can substantially reduce the return compared with national savings.

If you invest via unit trusts, capital gains are taxable if your gains from all investments for the year exceed £8000.

CHAPTER SUMMARY

- Monetary policy is conducted by the Bank of England. It is designed to influence the rate of growth in bank deposits and the exchange rate, in order to deliver economic objectives set by the Government.
- The principle tool of monetary policy is the rate of interest. The Bank of England sets the basic rate of interest by means of open market operations which change the amount of liquidity in the money market and its price. Others forms of control include reserve ratios, monetary base and capital ratios.

7 Linkages between the components of the system

RATES OF INTEREST, RATES OF RETURN, WEALTH, SAVINGS AND INVESTMENT

In this section we shall draw together some of the components of the economic system and show the linkages between them. But first some key principles.

Income is a stream of earnings and in its simplest form represents cash in our pocket. Wealth is an increase in the value (market price) of assets, held directly or indirectly. An example of direct holding would be ownership of a house; indirect would be owning shares in a property company.

The rate of interest indicates an income stream, the rate of return indicates a change in the value of wealth, not necessarily an income stream.

To illustrate: if you place £100 in a building society account, with a 10% rate of interest, after a year, you receive £10 (ignore tax). The rate of interest is 10% and the rate of return to you is also 10%.

If you purchased 100 shares in George Wimpey PLC for 100 pence each, your total outlay would be £100. Assume the dividend paid at the end of the year is 5 pence per share, what is the rate of return?

Assuming no change in the share price, the rate of return is

$$\frac{\text{Dividend in pence per share}}{\text{Market price per share}} = \frac{5p}{100p} = 5\%$$

This is known as the yield. It shows the cash return from ownership of the share.

What if the market price moves from 100 pence to 125 pence over the period of ownership, but the dividend remains the same? The yield falls from 5% to 4%. But the cash return is still the same.

Assuming a change in the share price, the rate of return is a different calculation. It takes into account the capital gain (or loss).

The share is purchased at 100 pence; market price now 125 pence. This is a capital gain of 25%. It is not a cash return (unless you sell the share). It is an increase in wealth.

The total return on the original stake of £100 will be a combination of cash (the dividend) and capital gain (the increase in wealth).

The total return is 25 pence per share capital gain plus 5 pence per share dividend, which together is 30%.

Over the whole business cycle, the total return on shares will exceed the return on fixed interest (Bonds) assuming you purchase at the bottom and sell close to the top.

It is common for investors to compare rates of interest payable in a building society account with the yield on shares to assess cash return; at a time of falling interest rates, shares become more attractive, because of their yield. But as the 'wall of money' flows from building society accounts to the stock market, yields fall.

However, many companies have a policy of maintaining yield at, say, 3.5%. If their share price is rising, so will the dividend payout rise in pence per share, to maintain yield.

Is the purchase of shares saving or investment?

If you, from your current income, decide to purchase shares this is saving. You'll expect a return on your saving. A company will issue new shares to finance its growth and the purchase of fixed assets (buildings, machinery). So if you purchase new shares, saving will equal investment. However if you purchase shares from someone else, you are saving, but there is no corresponding increase in investment. The seller of shares may be going liquid, selling for cash. Of course subsequently the seller may use (your) cash to purchase assets. There is an important dynamic here which has implications for the economy as a whole.

A share is a claim on a company's assets and its earnings. A company issues share capital in order to purchase assets, or invest in innovation, or to reduce its debt or re-equip its plant. A new issue provides cash to the company, and this cash is used by the directors to add value. Part of the added value is paid to the share holders as dividend, the rest is an indicator of how successful the company is, and this will tend to attract purchasers for the existing shares, thus bidding up the price.

The original share issue is a source of funds. Subsequent sales or purchases of existing shares have no direct impact on the company except that if the price is rising, the market capitalization in the value of the company will be rising and the current shareholders will feel wealthier.

A rising stock market is the result of more people wanting to own shares (demand) than there are shares available (supply). But everything has its price and as prices rise so some existing holders will sell (thus turning their wealth into cash – going liquid).

But why should people want to purchase shares?

1 Alternative forms of saving less attractive because of:
   (a) low (and falling) interest rates
   (b) rising inflation
   (c) companies promise increased dividend
   (d) expectations that share prices will continue to rise
2 Tax advantages e.g. Personal Equity Plans
3 Rising disposable incomes from already high levels produces 'spare funds'
4 Overseas investors find the domestic market 'cheap' if the currency has devalued. All other things equal, a 10% devaluation of sterling, against the dollar, makes the London market 10% more attractive than the USA. If a revaluation in the currency is expected, then in the future, the dividend stream will be worth more in $.

In Chapter 10 there is a section on the cyclical indicators. The FT 500 share index is a shorter leading indicator. An upturn in the index, all other things being equal, is followed by an upturn in GDP. Over 20 years the relationship has proved resilient.

One of the key drivers of share price is 'expected future stream of earnings' – in short, the dividend.

Dividend is a profits distribution. Under normal circumstances a Board has to decide its dividend policy, which results in a percentage of current earnings (measured as net profit) to be paid out in dividend and the rest retained in the business.

As a rule of thumb for the UK 40% is paid out, 60% is retained. This gives a dividend cover of 2.5 times. It means the total dividend could be paid out, 2.5 times over, from current profits.

If the market expects profits to rise sharply, a given dividend cover results in higher dividends. The market is buying a future income stream.

One main consideration is whether the share price represents good value or not. The price – earnings ratio (P/E) is one way of assessing this. The P/E is calculated as:

$$\frac{\text{Current share price}}{\text{earnings in pence per share}} \quad = \quad \text{Times}$$

Assume the share price is 200 pence, and the earnings per share (eps) which is $\dfrac{\text{net profit}}{\text{no. of shares in issue}}$

is 10p, then the P/E is $\dfrac{200}{10}$ = 20 times

If the share price increases, so will the P/E e.g. $\dfrac{300}{10}$ = 30 times

The significance of the P/E is that it is an indication of market confidence in a company. If someone is willing to pay twenty times most recent earnings, then in general, they will be anticipating a significant improvement over the next couple of years.

Of course, if a company announces a high dividend in pence per share, the P/E is likely to rise as the market buys in order to share in the income stream.

As a general rule, P/E in excess of 20 suggests high levels of optimism and below 8, pessimism. But this will vary between sectors. A cyclical stock (where eps is likely to rise and fall with the business cycle) e.g. construction will have high P/E at the start of the upturn (indeed there may be no P/E to calculate because the company made losses) and falling P/Es near the peak as the market sees future earnings likely to fall below historic.

A blue-chip stock is likely to have stable eps growth, and a stable P/E, say around 8–12. The expression 'blue-chip' is applied to those companies who through the cycle maintain their earnings, their dividend, and hence experience only small movements in their share price.

The data reproduced below is from the FT dated 22 March 1994.

	Month 21	Day's Change %	Year ago	Dividend Yield %	P/E Ratio
FTSE100	3198	−0.6	2863.9	3.78	20.40

The FTSE100, known as the Footsie 100, is an index of 100 companies. Mostly blue-chip, the right to be in the 100 is based on market capitalization (i.e. the value that the market places on the company. It is shares in issue × the current share price).

The index allows market makers to assess the performance of leading companies. In a year it has risen 10.4%. The dividend yield on average is 3.78%. The P/E at 20.40 indicates that the market is optimistic that the earnings (and dividend payout) of these 100 companies will improve over the next year or so.

The savings institutions

The savings institutions are financial intermediaries. In the UK they consist of banks, building societies, insurance companies and pension funds. Banks create credit, building societies accept deposits and parcel them up into loans, mostly for house purchase.

Insurance companies and pension funds accept money from customers today, and promise a return sometime in the future. The key challenge for the managers is to ensure that the portfolio of assets they purchase with their current cash will earn sufficient future cash to meet their liabilities, which are essentially pension payments.

The portfolio of assets could vary according to the fund managers' assessment of future earnings.

For example, in 1980 a typical fund would look like this:

10%	Cash
30%	UK equity
15%	Overseas equity
20%	Property
25%	Gilts

In 1991 it would have changed to this:

5%	Cash
60%	UK equity
25%	Overseas equity
5%	Property
5%	Gilts

In Germany, insurance companies buy Bonds (the German equivalent of gilts) and around 95% of their portfolio would consist of these. There is very little share ownership in Germany, either directly or indirectly. Only 5% of Germans own shares compared with 20% in the UK. All but 50 of Germany's 660 listed companies are majority controlled by other corporate shareholders.

One of the important drivers of share prices at a particular time in the year is the 'churning' activities of fund managers. They try and produce a fund which returns more than the market average by selling and repurchasing shares at a lower price, thus producing a portfolio gain.

THE BEHAVIOUR OF THE MONEY SUPPLY THROUGH THE BUSINESS CYCLE

The business cycle is the change in the volume of goods and services sold through time.

The money supply consists of narrow money (notes and coin) and broad money which is notes and coin plus bank deposits plus building society deposits.

Money is used as a store of wealth, for settlement of debt, to finance current assets (working capital) and capital assets (land, buildings and equipment).

It is also used as a medium of exchange.

GDP at current prices equals money times velocity.

A change in GDP at current prices is driven by changes in money times velocity.

Is narrow money M0 more important than broad money M4?

In volume terms M0 is insignificant. It comprises 4% of the total UK money supply M4. In a society where non-cash payments systems are highly developed, this is to be expected. In the UK most of the population use only notes and coin to purchase small ticket items. It is literally the small change of the system. The decision to hold notes and coin instead of bank deposits is a personal one. At a time when all bank deposits are interest bearing, to hold notes and coin results in a loss of interest. But at low interest rates this loss is negligible.

The rate of interest has an impact on the willingness to hold notes and coin or bank deposits. All other things being equal, when interest rates increase, people will switch from notes and coin to bank deposits.

Does this switch have any impact on spending? The best guess is no. Funds in a current account can just as easily be spent using a cheque book or Switch facility; the decision to spend is distinct from the decision to hold money and in which form.

But transactions technology does have an impact. If Switch or cheques are not widely accepted then more notes and coin will be used.

The rate of inflation and the expected rate of inflation may well have an impact. If prices are expected to rise people bring forward their purchase decision; the method of payment – notes and coin, cheque or Switch – is an irrelevance. Similarly, if prices are expected to fall, people may delay their purchase decision.

People can decide to hold their wealth in things of varying liquidity:

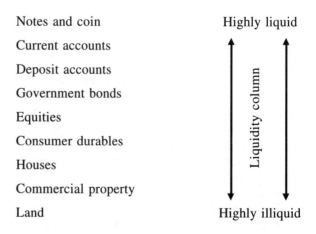

Notes and coin	Highly liquid
Current accounts	
Deposit accounts	
Government bonds	
Equities	
Consumer durables	
Houses	
Commercial property	
Land	Highly illiquid

Some significant entrepreneurs like Walter Goldsmith always 'go liquid' before the business cycle turns down. They move up the liquidity column. In doing so they sell assets for cash. This increases the amount of transactions.

Peter Oppenheimer, chief economic strategist at Hambros Bank, has watched the behaviour of the financial markets and produced a chart which is shown in Figure 7.1.

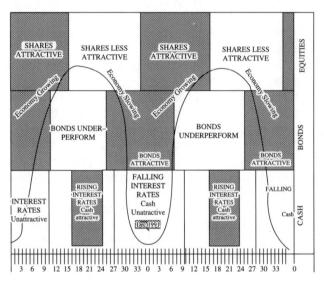

Figure 7.1 Behaviour of the financial markets

This analysis is based on a pattern measured since 1960. The pattern is set up as the result of the interplay of three variables: economic growth (real change in GDP) inflation rates (RPI) and interest rates.

The typical cycle repeats itself every three years (unless there is a shock like the Gulf War)

It is caused by people changing the way in which they manage their wealth (or rather fund managers who act on the individuals' behalf).

The behaviour of M4 through the cycle

Broad money M4 includes M0 – notes and coin. If people go liquid, and decide to increase their holding of notes and coin, then the proportion of M4 which is notes and coin increases, but the total amount of M4 remains the same; unless:

- People sell UK assets to overseas buyers who finance the purchase outside the UK (M4 goes up)
- Someone raises a bank loan in order to purchase the assets and the bank creates a deposit (M4 goes up).

An increase in M4 is an increase in bank liabilities, i.e. deposits. A bank's balance sheet must always balance. An increase in bank liabilities has its counterpart in increased assets, i.e. advances and loans.

The banking system can only increase its liabilities *if it first increases its advances*.

An increase in advance is the result of a bank and its customer agreeing an amount and a price (so many % above base rate).

An increase in advances increases broad money. The economic impact depends on what the customer does with this new deposit. He is unlikely to leave it on deposit (if he does, the impact is zero). Instead he will spend it. This is a *new* deposit, it causes an increase in nominal GDP when it is spent.

It follows that an increase in broad money, assuming no change in velocity and stable prices, will cause an equivalent increase in nominal GDP because unlike an increase in M0, an increase in M4 represents new money rather than a change in liquidity.

Planned vs. unplanned increases in M4

A planned increase in M4 is the result of individuals and companies going along to their bank to increase their holdings of deposits by asking for a loan or overdraft. It is planned because the use for the new deposit is anticipated. It's either to finance the purchase of an asset or to finance the growth of a business, i.e. to finance stocks and work in progress.

An unplanned increase in M4 is when individuals or companies are forced to increase their holding of deposits because events have not worked out as planned: sudden redundancy or a crashed car which was under-insured and needs replacing; stocks building because a major customer cancels an order at the last minute; or a major customer fails to pay your invoice on the due date.

Unplanned growth in M4 takes place at the beginning of an economic downswing. Take a look at Figure 7.2. This plots inflation adjusted M4, against inflation adjusted GDP and inflation adjusted Retail Sales. There was significant unplanned growth in M4 in 1989 and 1990 to finance an unplanned increase in unsold goods.

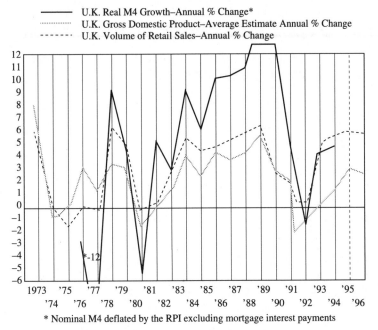

—————— U.K. Real M4 Growth–Annual % Change*
.... U.K. Gross Domestic Product–Average Estimate Annual % Change
- - - - - - U.K. Volume of Retail Sales–Annual % Change

* Nominal M4 deflated by the RPI excluding mortgage interest payments

Figure 7.2   Inflation adjusted M4, GDP and retail sales

It is also the case that if prices rise faster than companies expect, then the level of short term finance required is higher than expected. Under these circumstances there is an unplanned increase in M4.

The worst case scenario is 'Slumpflation', where an unplanned slowdown plus rising prices requires substantial new deposits to finance activity. This was the German situation in 1992/93, and was the UK situation in 1989/90.

CHAPTER SUMMARY

■ There is a difference between wealth and income. Wealth is not cash; income is.

- The rate of return on an asset can be considered from an income perspective (the yield) or a capital gain perspective (the return).
- As people adjust their personal portfolios there is an impact on the number of transactions in the economy and the liquidity of the system.
- One of the key elements of the system is broad money M4 and the extent to which changes in its level are planned or unplanned. A change in liquidity can affect both the level of M4 and its constituents.

8 The balance of payments and trade

THE UK BALANCE OF PAYMENTS

The Balance of Payments is a set of accounts which measures the value, in sterling, of all transactions between people resident in the UK and others.

The method of accounting is by double-entry. There are always errors and omissions, so a balancing item ensures that the sum of credits matches the sum of the debits. The principles of double-entry require this and so in bookkeeping terms, each month and each year the UK Balance of Payments must balance.

We shall be exploring some of the ways in which this balance is achieved. In Table 8.1 you will see a summary of the accounts for 1987. Each component has a letter against it, referred to in the text.

A   The balance of trade

This is the difference between the value of visible exports and the value of visible imports. The UK usually has a deficit on the trade balance, except when the economy slows down rapidly or, as between 1979 and 1985, the price and volume of oil exports has resulted in surpluses.

In 1987, there was a deficit of £10.1 billion. This was due to the rapid growth in the volume of raw materials, manufactured and semi-manufactured items imported as UK domestic demand grew strongly.

Table 8.1 UK balance of payments 1989 £ million					
DEBITS		**CREDITS**		**MOVEMENTS**	
Current Account					
Visible		Visible		negative trade	
Imports	89.5	Exports	79.4	balance	(A)
Invisible		Invisible		surplus on	
Imports	72.4	Exports	80.0	invisibles	(B)
	161.9		159.4	current	
				account deficit	(C)
Capital Account					(D)
Short term		Short term			
Capital out	47	capital in	68		(E)
Long term		Long term		Surplus on	
investment out	15	investment in	6	capital account	(F)
	62		74		
Addition to		Withdrawal			
reserves	12	from reserves	0	12 to reserves	(G)
Totals	235.9		233.4		(H)
Balancing item	0		2.5	+2.5 balancing item	(I)
UK Balance of Payments	235.9		235.9	Zero	(J)

B   The invisibles

Invisibles are mainly the value of service transactions. They include the flow of interest, profits and dividends from overseas investments. In 1987 the UK enjoyed a surplus of £7.6 billion on this account.

C   The current balance

The current account is not the trade balance, nor is it the balance of payments. It is the balance of trade plus net invisibles. In the trough of the business cycle, it tends to be in surplus; towards the peak of the cycle, it tends to be in deficit.

As the accounts must balance, a deficit on the current account has to be financed by a corresponding surplus on the capital account. Conversely, if there is a surplus on the current account, there must be a deficit of an equal value on the capital account.

D The capital account

The Capital Account measures money flows in and out of the UK and to and from reserves held by the Bank of England.

E Short-term capital movements

The largest of the money flows and also the most volatile are called Short-term capital movements (SCMs). The official title is 'portfolio and other investment flows' and SCMs are also part of banking flows to and from the UK.

The SCMs are basically the result of international movements in liquidity. This liquidity moves between world financial centres in search of the highest rate of return commensurate with a pre-determined risk. The risk comes from likely swings in the exchange value of international currencies and changes in international interest rate differentials, which causes bond prices to move.

Because SCMs are so volatile, they can be used to finance a current account deficit, providing the Treasury allows the Bank of England to raise UK interest rates far enough. Because SCMs are money flows, the exchange rate in the short-term is largely determined by them; since global financial deregulation began in 1979, this is increasingly the case.

F Long-term investment

These are money flows in and out of the UK. They are not interest rate or exchange rate sensitive. They are the result of the increasing globalization of business. For example, when Toyota decide to build an assembly plant in Derbyshire, the funds for this come through this part of the account. Conversely, if ICI decide to re-equip a plant in the USA and the funds are provided from London, there is an outflow.

G   Reserves

The Bank of England operates the Exchange Equalization Account. Through this account, it buys and sells sterling using a number of foreign exchange brokers.

An addition to the reserves is shown as a debit entry. This is because the Bank of England is selling sterling in exchange for, say, US dollars. The Bank receives dollars, the market receives sterling. Reserves of dollars increase, the sterling goes abroad. The effect is identical to a transaction where a UK resident sells sterling for dollars to purchase an American export. In both cases, sterling leaves the country.

In the example, the Bank of England has added £12 billion to the reserves. This means that it has intervened in the foreign exchange market, selling sterling for other currencies. The reason for this was to prevent sterling from gaining value against other currencies, thus helping exporters to maintain their profit margins.

H   As you might expect, when the Government is measuring huge, diverse flows there will be errors and omissions and the accounts don't balance.

I   The balancing item

This is used to produce a balance. The fiddle factor. It can be very large, either positive or negative and is adjusted through time as statistical errors are eliminated. In 1986, the balancing item was a staggering £11,727 billion. In 1987 it happened, at £2.5 billion, to be equivalent to the current account deficit.

J   As stated at the beginning, the accounts must balance and the final figure is the UK balance of payments, £235.9 billion. This represents 56% of GDP at current prices, but for the economy as a whole this figure is pretty meaningless. What matters is the share of GDP which is spent on imports and provided by exports.

In the 1980s, exports averaged 28% of GDP and imports 30% of GDP. Over 50% of UK exports are to EC countries, about 30% to the USA and the remainder to the rest of the world. Exports of manufactured items still earn more than 55% of export revenues.

The UK balance of payments 1987–94

From 1987 import volumes steadily diverged from export volumes and the gap increased. In the first quarter of 1989, export volumes were up 11%, but import volumes were up 17% on the same period in 1988. This is because:

1 In 1988 there was a rapid increase in UK investment (up 14% on 1987) not matched by the same increase in savings. The difference came from abroad, through the capital account.
2 The UK can only supply a limited range of products to world markets at competitive prices, quality and design. Whenever domestic demand surges, imports grow faster than exports.
3 The strengthening of sterling, particularly against the dollar, reduced price competitiveness.
4 There was a shortage of domestic productive capacity for supply to both home and overseas markets.

From 1992, the gap between import volumes and export volumes narrowed sharply, because:

1 UK investment fell and domestic savings rose.
2 The devaluation of sterling after leaving the ERM in October 1992 increased price competitiveness.
3 There was a surplus of productive capacity.

The current account deficit

In 1989, the deficit was 3% of GDP. But because of global financial deregulation and current account surpluses in Japan and West Germany, the British deficit was easily financed, assuming that corporate treasurers saw that the return (rate of interest) was commensurate with the risk.

It is likely that a deficit of not more than 2–3% can always be financed, if it remains stable.

Are services the way out?

Financial and services sector activity does not provide sufficient export earnings to pay for our imports. Nor is it likely to.

In 1988 the City earned £4.6 billion in fees and other charges from overseas. Investment earnings from overseas contributed another £7.3 billion. Consultancy export earnings were £1.3

billion. This gives a total of £13.2 billion compared with manu-facturing exports of £90.6 billion the same year.

In 1991, the UK exported £103Bn of goods and £31Bn of services. It imported £113Bn of goods and £26Bn of services. There was a deficit of £10Bn on goods and a surplus of £5Bn on services, thus giving a current account deficit of £5Bn. But it remains that exports of goods provide 70% of our overseas income and 24% of our total income.

WHY DO COUNTRIES TRADE?

The underlying basis for trade is the principle of comparative advantage.

The principle of comparative advantage

Adam Smith in the *Wealth of Nations*, published in 1776, argued that if one of two countries could produce one product at lower cost, and the other, a second product at lower cost; each country would benefit from trade. From this idea the principle of absolute advantage evolved.

David Ricardo in the *Principles of Political Economy and Taxation* (1821) showed that it was comparative advantage (not absolute advantage) which mattered.

Let us take Ricardo's example. He considered cloth and wine, comparing England and Portugal. These figures show the hours of labour required to produce a certain quantity of each:

	Cloth	Wine
England	100	120
Portugal	90	80

From the figures Portugal has the absolute advantage in wine and cloth. Is there any basis for trade?

Portugal can produce wine using 33% less labour than the UK; and cloth using 10% less labour. Portugal has a comparative advantage in wine. England has a comparative advantage in cloth (not an absolute advantage). England can produce cloth using 111% of the hours required in Portugal ($\frac{100}{90}$) but to produce wine would use 150% ($\frac{120}{80}$) of the hours required in Portugal.

Each country would gain if England specialized in cloth for 80 hours of labour and wine for 100 hours. This assumes that the international price ratio was 1 unit of cloth = 1 unit of wine. It also assumes perfect competition in all markets.

The exchange rate and domestic price levels can influence the degree of comparative advantage.

Today, the Terms of Trade is an important index. It is the ratio of the price of exports to imports. It represents the import purchasing power of a given volume of exports.

A rise in the terms of trade is an improvement. It enables more imports to be purchased, for an unchanged volume of exports.

For example:

Unit value of Exports	Unit value of Imports	Terms of Trade	$\frac{A}{B} \times 100$
47.6	41.1	115.9	
50.8	42.8	118.8	
53.7	44.8	119.8	
100	100	100	
119.6	122.1	98.0	

The principle of comparative advantage applies to changes in relative prices. Changes in relative prices can come about via changes in the exchange rate, applied technology, productivity or tariffs.

Free trade pros and cons

The principle

Trade and specialization are intimately connected. Without trade everyone must be self-sufficient, with trade everyone can specialize.

International trade, under conditions of free competition enables each country to specialize according to the principle of comparative advantage. Inefficient industries contract and release factors of production for the efficient industries. In this way, prices are kept in line with the costs of the most efficient industries and consumers benefit from lower prices.

It sounds good, but many contemporary economists are reluctant to support free trade because of two basic concerns:

1   The real world does not operate free markets.
2   There is no necessary relationship between free trade and greater welfare.

A free market depends on the model of perfect competition. Under these conditions there is no monopoly, oligopoly, advertising, special promotion, penetration pricing, loss leading, no ignorance, no uncertainty, no risk and perfect mobility of factors of production (a miner can become a computer software expert without difficulty). The model implicitly assumes that there is no divergence between price and social cost and benefit – market prices reflect the true opportunity costs of production. The true opportunity cost is the cost of the next best alternative good where all pollution costs are taken fully into account.

The real world is different. Most man-made products are sold under conditions of oligopoly, there is international competition amongst the few, trade takes place accompanied by all the tricks, pressures and campaigns of companies. In short, prices are not determined by the costs of the most efficient. Free trade under such conditions does not necessarily bring about great efficiency.

By altering relative prices, free trade also alters income distribution within nations and between nations. It is not at all evident that what some groups gain from free trade outweighs what other groups, e.g. the unemployed or the extremely poor, lose from free trade. In short, because markets are not free, governments often intervene in order to protect those sectors of society which would lose as a result.

World trade and GATT

World trade is big business. In 1989, 57% of world trade was manufactured goods by value, 11% agriculture, 9.5% mining and the rest services.

In 1947, 24 countries signed the General Agreement on Tariffs and Trade (GATT). Since then 64 countries have joined.

Up until 1973, the volume of world trade grew each year. The first oil shock in November 1973 affected the non-oil developing countries substantially. Import prices rose sharply into deficit on current accounts. The current problem of third world debt is a direct result of the imbalances set up in the 1970s – the beginning of the seventies saw a dramatic rise in commodity prices. The

Regional composition
of world merchandise
exports 1989
Percentage share based on value data

Composition
of world trade 1989
Percentage share based on value data

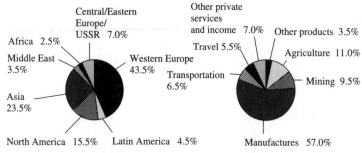

Figure 8.1   World trade

export revenues of non-industrial countries rose sharply. This was
reversed from 1975. 1973–79 saw sharp rises in the oil revenue of
oil exporting countries, with the consequential surpluses.

The growth of barter

The recession in developing countries, the oil glut and sharp
fluctuations in exchange rates are causing a rise in counter trade,
the official term for barter. It is estimated that in 1982 30% of
world trade was barter. In 1991, British Aerospace was supplying
fighter aircraft to the Saudis and being paid in oil.

The main advantages:

1   Reduces need for foreign exchange.
2   Emphasizes bilateral agreements – gives a developing country
    a chance to gain access to a western market.
3   Under 'compensation' arrangements countries can acquire vital
    technology and plant in return for a proportion of their output.

The European Community – EC

The EC is a common market; it has eliminated internal customs
duties, thus enabling manufacturers to treat the whole EC as their
domestic market. The Common External Tariff (CET) is applied
on goods entering the EC – once in they can circulate without
further tariff.

The EC accounts for one third of world exports, more than the USA and Japan together. Exports are on average equal to 25% of GDP of member countries (compared with 10% for the USA and 18% for Japan). 55% of EC trade is between member states, a further 5% with neighbours in EFTA, the European Free Trade Association – Norway, Iceland, Switzerland and Finland see Table 8.2.

No internal tariffs exist but there were still a whole variety of non-tariff barriers to block trade in existence in the mid-eighties. Many of these have been removed as a result of increased efforts by the EC.

For example:

- Dutch lorry drivers had to obtain 300 separate rubber stamps to get a lorry load of Gouda cheese into France.
- For a time, all video cassettes imported to France had to be cleared at customs in Poitiers, miles from ports of entry and staffed by eight men.
- All French customs papers must now be written in French.
- Health regulations in Germany effectively prevented the French exporting mineral water.
- Bavarian brewery laws effectively prevented the sale of other European beers in Bavaria.

The impact of North Sea Oil on the UK

The effect of oil on the Balance of Payments is as follows:

1   The Current Account: visible exports increase.
    North Sea Oil is high quality, it is mixed with lower grade imported oil, leaving a large higher priced surplus for export.
2   Repatriation of interest, profit and dividend.
    Foreign oil companies produce 50% of North Sea oil. They hold 60% of the exploration rights. They have invested twice as much as UK companies. Now they are taking their reward which counts as a debit item on visible trade, whether or not the funds actually go overseas. If the profits are retained in the UK, it shows up as a capital inflow (on the capital account). In 1985 interest, profit and dividend was 16% of the value of oil and gas production.
3   Capital inflows to develop North Sea reserves. These are a capital account item. Shown as a credit, they were particularly heavy in the mid-1970s, now a lot less but still positive.

Table 8.2   Companies deriving at least 20% of trading profits from the EC (Excluding UK)

	% Profits		% Profits		% Profits
TIP Europe	56	BBA	30	TDG	22
Unilever	50	Manpower	30	Cadbury Schweppes	21
Queens Moat	49	Glaxo	29	MB	21
Hazelwood Foods	42	De La Rue	28	Allied-Lyons	20
RMC	41	Steetley	28	British Aerospace	20
Wolseley	37	BPB	27	Fisons	20
T&N	36	IMI	25	Dawson	20
Lucas	35	Siebe	25	Lowe	20
Thorn EMI	35	British Steel	25	Saatchi	20
GKN	34	APV	24	Vickers	20
SK Beecham	33	Pilkington	24	WPP	20
Redland	32	GEC	22	Scottish & Newcastle	20
TI Group	30	Guinness	22		

Source: S.G. Warburg October 1990

The Treasury estimates that the net effect of North Sea Oil was as follows:

	1980	1981	1982	1983	1984	1985
% GDP	3.5	4.5	4.75	5.5	5	4

The changing nature of UK trade and payments

The development of trade is crucial for the UK economy. In 1984 29% of UK domestic product was exported. In the same year the figure for France was 21%, Germany 26%, Italy 25%, USA 9%, Canada 25% and Japan 13%. The figure for the UK in 1960 was 20%.

Since 1970 there have been significant structural changes in the UK's visible trade, both the EC and North Sea oil have had an impact. Since the war the old colonies have become less important, and Europe more so.

The changing structure of UK exports and imports (as a % of total trade):

		Exports	Imports
Food, Drink, Tobacco and basic raw materials	1963	12	47
	1972	8	30
	1982	23	25
Manufacturing	1963	62	27
	1972	58	42
	1982	51	52
Services	1963	26	27
	1972	31	26
	1982	24	20

Source: Bank of England Quarterly Bulletin, December 1983

North Sea Oil and the adjustment process

In 1957 the Dutch discovered vast supplies of natural gas close to their border with Germany. Subsequently, this gas was sold to Germany. The result: an upward movement in the exchange rate for the Dutch Guilder, and a decline in Dutch manufacturing capacity. As the principle of comparative advantage would predict: the Dutch found comparative advantage in gas. They exported gas and imported manufactures. When the gas ran out in 1979, the Dutch were forced to run an austerity programme 'Bestek 80' cutting imports and trying to restore comparative advantage in the manufacturing sector.

This example from Holland was closely followed by the UK experience.

The Balance of Payments are recorded by double-entry. As a result, each month the accounts must balance. What is of interest is the way in which the balance is achieved. If there is a surplus of income over expenditure then the surplus can be lent overseas or added to the reserves. If there is a deficit, this can be covered by borrowing from overseas or withdrawals from the reserves. If there is a persistent imbalance (surplus or deficit) some form of adjustment is required.

Adjustment can take place on the CURRENT account or the CAPITAL account or both. It can be AUTOMATIC or DISCRETIONARY.

Automatic adjustment comes about as the result of prevailing economic forces. Most common is a change in the exchange value of sterling.

Discretionary adjustment is the result of policy actions which can reduce expenditure or switch expenditure.

AUTOMATIC ADJUSTMENT

The optimists maintain that a balance of payments deficit is a transient phenomena. Automatically, forces come into play which will reduce it. There are basically three components:

1   A deficit is the result of expenditure being greater than income. Assume a fixed exchange rate. Domestic demand will fall, thus reducing the demand for the volume of imports. The deflationary effect causes prices or wages to fall, thus making exports cheaper, which tends to increase their volume.
2   Assume a fixed exchange rate. If wages and prices do not fall, incomes will, as lower demand employs less people, thus the demand for imports falls.

3   If the exchange rate is allowed to fall, then exports would be relatively cheaper and imports relatively more expensive. In theory export volumes should increase, import volumes fall.

Between 1971 and 1990 and since September 1992 we have lived under conditions of floating exchange rates and so we now consider item 3 above and the effects of a devaluation of sterling.

Assume an exporter from the UK sets an export price of £100. At £1 = $1.80, the selling price in dollars is $180.

Assume now the pound falls to £1 = $1.40. If our exporter sells at $180 he makes a big increase in profit per unit, because he now will receive $180, which when exchanged into £ will be £128 – a 28% increase in profit.

But our exporter has a choice; he could sell the goods at $140 and receive the same number of pounds per unit as before (£100) and probably increase his sales volume because his price has fallen in dollar terms 22%. Or he could reduce the US price by, say, 11% and gain more volume and greater profit per unit.

Thus a devaluation of sterling makes importing more profitable and encourages larger volumes. This applies to invisibles as well as visibles. It also makes imports relatively more expensive and encourages people to holiday at home (and foreigners to come here for holidays.)

A devaluation makes exporting more profitable particularly in the short run. Over the long run (more than 18 months) the rise in import prices can quickly cause wage-push, and rising unit labour costs, thus eroding margins from the cost-push side.

The 'J' curve

One of the characteristics of UK trade is that exports are more price sensitive than imports. This has important results following devaluation. Devaluation increases the UK's import bill overnight. The revenue from exports is initially unchanged, so the trade balance worsens. But, in time, high priced imports are gradually replaced by lower priced home-produced goods (so the theory goes) and the balance of trade gradually improves.

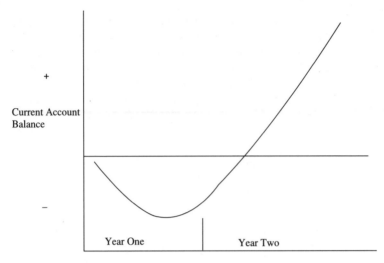

Figure 8.2 The 'J' curve

Import controls – pros and cons

The cons

1 Import controls of whatever type undermine free trade and therefore, according to the principle of comparative advantage, reduce the level of efficiency of the global system (bear in mind the counter argument.)
2 Import controls may induce retaliation from those countries which find their exports reduced.
3 Import controls may be unfair, unless applied across the board.
4 The belief that import controls will stimulate domestic production and employment may be misguided. Import controls only work if domestic producers expand their production of goods formerly imported, and maintain their production of goods for export. The protagonist assumes that domestic producers have the inclination and the ability to produce substitutes.

The pros

In specific circumstances import controls are preferential to free trade, particularly if it leads to a rapid rise in unemployment and mass closures of companies.

In 1979, the Thatcher Government abolished foreign exchange controls. Real interest rates rose, the rate of growth in Government spending was reduced and in June 1979 the price of oil increased 200%. The combined effect was to push up the value of sterling. What is the effect of a rapid revaluation?

Assume our exporter sets an export price of £100 when the exchange value of sterling is £1 = $1.80 and subsequently the value changes to £1 = $2.40. The USA price of the product rises from £1.80 to $2.40. An increase of 33%.

Our exporter has a choice; he can push the price to $2.40 and suffer a sharp volume fall and a fall in total profit (although unit profit will be the same). Or he can increase the price by, say, 10% to $1.98 and suffer a reduction in unit profit. At $1.98, the sterling return is £82.50. Unless the product enjoys a huge margin, this price will be unprofitable.

THE BALANCE OF PAYMENTS IN A STATISTICAL BLACK HOLE

The balancing item is almost as big as the UK current account deficit.

UK CURRENT ACCOUNT											
	'79*	'80*	'81*	'82	'83	'84	'85	'86	'87	'88	'89
Current a/c balance	−0.45	2.84	6.75	4.65	3.79	1.83	2.75	0.00	−4.18	−15.15	−19.12
Net fin transactions	−0.74	−3.94	−7.43	−2.59	−4.65	−7.92	−7.24	−8.51	0.47	7.01	4.00
Balancing item	1.00	0.91	0.53	−2.06	0.76	6.09	4.49	8.54	3.71	8.13	15.12

* figures include allowance for allocation in the national accounts or special drawing rights
Source: Central Statistical Office

About £15bn a year in Britain's overseas transactions does not show up in the Government's accounts.

The missing billions are thought to reflect either underestimates of capital flowing into Britain or unrecorded overseas sales by UK companies. The concern is that by not having the relevant information the UK Government is losing track over a vital area of data related to trade policy.

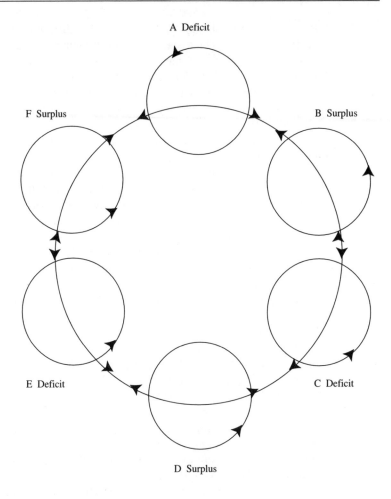

$$A+B+C+D+D+E+F=0$$

Figure 8.3 The global system of payments

The UK's statistical hole constitutes a large chunk of the £50Bn which, according to International Monetary Fund estimates, cannot be accounted for out of total global exports of £2,500Bn a year.

In Britain's case, the concern is heightened both because of the size of the statistical discrepancy and because of its relevance to Britain's large current account deficit, which at £19Bn in 1989 was the biggest in Europe, although it has fallen steadily since then.

Basic economic theory dictates that the difference between exports and imports for a specific country should be matched by currency flows of the same amount, much of it representing borrowing. The £50Bn global number represents the total value of exports where the transfer of goods in one direction cannot be matched by recorded monetary flows the other way.

Virtually all countries have statistical discrepancies in their trade figures. But Britain's is particularly large and grew considerably in the eighties.

For 1989, when the UK current account deficit was £19Bn, officials at the government's Central Statistical Office (CSO) identified net transfers into Britain of only about £4Bn.

That leads to the discrepancy of £15Bn – which economists call the balancing item.

The CSO collects its data from a number of sources, such as customs records, surveys of industrial and consumer spending and stock exchange accounts.

The appearance of such a large balancing item is thought to be due to a number of factors:

■ It may be due to sales overseas of services – part of Britain's invisible exports – which the government does not know about. Unrecorded sales of this kind could mean Britain's current account deficit could be smaller than thought.

■ Short-term capital inflows via the foreign exchange and bond markets – overseas traders buying pounds for speculative reasons – might be significantly larger than the government has a record of. These inflows could be pulled out at short notice, collapsing the exchange rate.

■ British residents could be importing to Britain large amounts of capital, arising from interest or rents on foreign assets, which they are failing to declare to the Inland Revenue.

■ The government might be failing to count some exports of manufactured items. Although figures for such visible trade are more reliable than those for invisibles, mistakes can happen. An oversight by customs officers led to Britain's national accounts between 1987 and 1990 failing to record aircraft imports worth about £1.5Bn.

■ The transfer of capital into Britain could be linked to criminal activities, such as the narcotics trade.

- Borrowing by UK institutions and individuals from overseas groups might be much greater than has been thought.

The CSO points out, in defence of the large discrepancy, that it is the residual number after adding and subtracting very large numbers in the annual accounts. Britain's exports and imports amount to £200Bn a year and the amount of capital swapped with overseas partners by UK-based foreign-exchange dealers every year runs to trillions of dollars.

In efforts to shed light on the hole in the accounts, the CSO recently found it had underestimated the value of UK equities which overseas residents and institutions bought during the 1980s. That accounted for capital inflows of about £1.5Bn a year which no one knew about.

As a result of this and other revisions, the CSO reduced its estimate of the balancing item for 1988, from £12Bn to £8Bn.

To discover more about unrecorded earnings the CSO has started a survey into details of overseas earnings from 25,000 UK services companies.

The balancing items undermine general confidence in the accuracy of the UK's financial statistics. Some would like to see the UK do more to track transfers of capital, such as occur when foreigners buy British equities or bonds. Others, however, say such ideas would be too bureaucratic and would be against the spirit of financial deregulation in post–1992 Europe.

Despite the problems of measurement, the system of double-entry bookkeeping requires that the sum of the global balances of payments is zero. One country's surplus is another country's deficit. This is illustrated in Figure 8.3.

CHAPTER SUMMARY

- The Balance of Payments as a set of double-entry books must always balance. A balance of payments problem exists when the balance is achieved through significant capital flows, particularly if they are short-term.
- The sum of the global balance of payments by definition is zero; one country's surplus is another country's deficit.
- The basis of trade is comparative advantage. Free trade in principle allows each country to maximize. Its growth by

exporting things in which it has comparative advantage and importing things which it has not.

- The EC as a customs union is designed to allow each member to expand according to comparative advantage.
- For all countries the Balance of Payment figures are inaccurate, particularly in the invisible earnings section.

9 International linkages: the exchange rate and international money flows

THE EXCHANGE RATE AND INTERNATIONAL MONEY FLOWS

Exchange rates are the price of one country's money in terms of another. They are determined by the willingness and ability of holders of currency A to exchange it for currency B, where holders of currency B are willing and able to supply currency B. If people are willing and able to supply more of A's currency it falls in terms of B.

The foreign exchange market which determines the price of currencies in terms of each other is dynamic: small changes in volumes can cause considerable swings in relative prices within a few minutes. As information technology and telephone links round the world have improved and countries have deregulated their markets, the daily flows of tradable currency have increased dramatically. About $180 Bn each day is traded in London. Indeed, in today's world, relative exchange rates are determined by international capital flows and investors' expectations, not by the trade in goods and services.

From 1949–1971, under the Bretton Woods agreement, the major international currencies were fixed against each other and the Dollar. Each country agreed to maintain the value of its currency within 1% of a fixed rate against the Dollar. This rate could only be changed if a country's balance of payments was in fundamental disequilibrium i.e. chronic deficit or massive surplus on the current account. A reduction in the rate is called devaluation, an increase in the rate, revaluation. The system broke down in 1971 when Nixon announced that the dollar would be allowed to float. 'Floating' is when a currency value changes in the foreign exchange markets without central bank intervention.

Under floating exchange rates, domestic monetary policy is reflected in the price of the currency. Countries with expansionary monetary policies (low interest rates) and rising inflation would suffer steady depreciation in the value of their currency. Countries with contractionary monetary policies (high interest rates) and lower inflation would experience an appreciating currency, as a general rule.

In the seventies and eighties nominal exchange rates have been volatile, and the real exchange rate much less stable than under the Bretton Woods arrangement.

Nominal exchange rates have moved perversely. Countries with high current account deficits and relatively high inflation have experienced strengthening currencies, e.g. the USA. From 1980 to 1985, the dollar rose 30% against the yen, and 76% against the DMark. This had a dramatic impact on the international price competitiveness of US industry, and the current account deteriorated further.

Rudiger Dornbusch of MIT has argued that because the foreign exchange market is efficient, then large swings in exchange rates must occur.

Here are the theories:

Purchasing Power Parity (PPP)

This theory says that exchange rates will move to equate the prices of internationally traded goods, i.e. so that $100 buys as much in the USA as a $100 of yen buys in Japan.

The PPP theory suggests that exchange rates should reflect relative inflation rates. If America's inflation rate is 6% and Japan's is 3%, then the dollar should fall 3% against the yen each year, to maintain PPP.

The monetary approach

This approach to exchange rates suggests that exchange rates are determined by differences in the rate of growth in the domestic money supply. If the USA doubles its money supply compared to the Japanese, then the dollar will be worth 50% less in terms of the yen.

The asset-market approach

This assumes that capital flows are more important than trade flows in determining exchange rates. In other words, it is the capital account (particularly short-term capital movements) which determines exchange rates, not the current account (i.e. trade flows). It is argued that corporate return from each currency (i.e. interest + expected depreciation or appreciation of the currency) must be equal.

So if yen deposits pay 5%, while dollar deposits pay 10%, the dollar will strengthen until it reaches a level from which investors expect it to depreciate by 5% in a year against the yen.

Thus exchange rates will change when interest rate differentials change OR WHEN EXPECTATIONS ABOUT FUTURE EXCHANGE RATES CHANGE.

The current view

This is a mixture of the PPP and the Asset Market Approach. In the long run exchange rates are determined by PPP, in the short run by interest rates and expectations.

If an investor sells some shares, his bank gains a deposit equal to the net sale price, the person who purchases the shares 'loses' a bank deposit of equivalent amount. Providing both individuals are UK residents, the total amount of money (bank deposits) is *unchanged*. Here we have a change in the level of transactions with no change in the volume of money. Therefore velocity of money must have risen.

Does a change in the volume of M0 have any impact on the level of economic activity?

This is a fundamental question. The answer is by no means clear. However, a change in M0 is coincident with a change (in the same direction) in retail sales.

If M0 goes up, it is because people are holding more of their income or wealth in notes and coin. The total amount of money hasn't changed, only its form.

When people demand more notes and coin, their banks draw it from the Central bank. The Central bank debits the drawing bank's current account by the amount, and credits its own banking account by the same amount. Thus the amount of bank deposits is the same as before but their form has changed from book entry to legal tender.

More notes and coin are in circulation, but the overall money supply is the same as before.

It is fair to conclude that figures for M0 are an expression of people's desire for liquidity and if there is no change in interest rates, expectations, or payments technology then the impact of M0 on economic activity is zero.

A currency can overshoot or undershoot its PPP value. Consider this scenario. If the clearing banks unexpectedly expand the money supply, prices will begin to rise, but if the real money supply is greater than before, interest rates will drop. Investors in sterling have rational expectations, they know that UK prices must eventually rise to the full extent of the increase in the money supply and that sterling must depreciate. They will require higher interest rates for holding sterling assets. Sterling will still depreciate but to less than its long-term value; at some point investors will expect it to appreciate and the appreciation will give them compensation for lower sterling interest rates. In this case sterling *undershoots*.

An unexpected tightening of the money supply (clearing banks reduce their lending) raises interest rates, and sterling *overshoots*, to a point at which the expected depreciation would just offset the rise in interest rates.

The ERM

The Exchange Rate Mechanism requires that in the long-term member Governments co-ordinate their economic policies, otherwise wide swings in interest rates will occur, because the ERM mechanism prevents the currency from achieving the necessary adjustment.

The myth of economic sovereignty

Since 1979 every industrial country including Japan has more of its economy under the control of foreign firms. The world is gradually becoming integrated as a result of foreign direct investment (FDI).

It is difficult to assess the impact of FDI because each country measures it in a different way. In the USA, owning 10% or more constitutes direct control. In Germany it is 25% and in France and the UK 20%. Acquisitions financed in the host country are not counted as direct investments.

Foreign ownership varies widely, as you can see from the chart.

Japan	1% of assets	0.4% of workforce
USA	9% of assets	4.0% of workforce
UK	14% of assets	14.0% of workforce
Germany	17% of assets	N/A
France	approx. 20% of assets	N/A

America has been the biggest recipient of new foreign investment. In the period 1980–1988, $250 Bn at 1980 prices flowed into the USA. Since 1988, $41 Bn per year has flowed in. America's assets abroad are worth less than foreigners' assets in America.

These figures suggest that freedom of capital will cause it to flow to areas where the highest return is possible over the longer term. It lets companies exploit their comparative advantage. A study by Graham and Kingman showed that foreign companies in the USA spend more on R & D and pay equivalent wages compared with the locals.

FDI flows over the last decade have caused economists to suggest that the current account deficit on a nation's balance of payments no longer reflects how well the local firms are doing. For example, when Texas Instruments sells a chip from its plant in Singapore to its US parent, this counts as an import.

In 1986 it is estimated that 33% of US exports were purchased by US companies based abroad. 20% of US imports were purchased from US owned companies abroad.

Foreign Direct Investment is becoming a major factor in the development of the global system. In effect, freedom of capital is forcing countries to compete for investment by offering superior infrastructure, quality of life, skilled labour forces, tax breaks and stability in exchange rates.

The general agreement on trade and tariffs

One of the biggest obstacles to the development of world trade is a history of trade barriers, quotas and tariffs, based on local protectionism. In 1945, tariffs on international trade averaged 40%. In 1975 the figure was 5%.

Reduction in tariffs and the freeing up of trade is a key pre-requisite for international capital flows and the improvement of each country's international competitiveness. Protectionism prevents competition, it dulls a country's determination to upgrade its industry and commerce.

Exchange rate volatility in the first half of 1991

In mid-February 1991 the dollar was DM 1.443. By Easter (30 March) it had risen 18%, producing DM1.755. The surge reflected a shift in investor sentiment in favour of the USA following the end of the Gulf War, the rising doubt about the stability of Germany following unification, and the inflow of funds as countries paid their contributions for the US war effort.

When investors' sentiment is neutral, the dominant impact on exchange rates is relative interbank (3 month) interest rates. The dollar surge began after US and German official discount rates (the effective rate of interest at which central banks supply liquidity [cash] to the domestic money market) crossed over at 6.5%, the US on the way down, the German on the way up. With neutral short run interest rates, animal spirits can take over. The pension funds found the US equity market cheap after a protracted fall in the dollar. Others found the German situation too cloudy to stay put.

Annual ranges for the US$ against the D-Mark, in pfennigs	
1985	100
1986	55
1987	35
1988	34
1989	34
1990	25
1991*	27

* first quarter

Source: Swiss Bank Corp, London

This switch wrong-footed the interbank traders and the chartists (who try to assess future exchange rate trends on the basis of existing movements).

In the early 1970s the western world was hit by the oil price shock and the collapse of the Bretton Woods system of fixed exchange rates. Economic policy co-ordination of the G7 (USA, Japan, Germany, Italy, UK, France and Canada) emerged since 1986 as a key factor influencing foreign exchange and markets. Since that year there has been co-ordinated currency intervention. The Louvre Accord in February 1987 involved massive intervention which may have triggered the October stock market crash.

Table 9.1 Foreign exchange market turnover and foreign trade

FOREIGN EXCHANGE MARKET TURNOVER AND FOREIGN TRADE April 1989 ($bn)		
Country	Net turnover (monthly total)	Foreign Trade[1]
United Kingdom	3,740	54.4
United States	2,580	101.6
Japan	2,300	61.5
Switzerland	1,140	13.7
Singapore	1,100	8.0[2]
Hong Kong	931	12.0[2]
Australia	570	9.7
France	520	44.3
Canada	300	25.0
Netherlands	260	22.9

[1] Monthly average for first quarter. [2] Exports and Imports of goods, April 1989.
Source: Bank for International Settlements

Foreign Exchange Market,
net average
daily turnover ($bn)

	March 1986	April 1989
UK	90.0	187.0
US	58.5	128.9
Japan	48.0	115.0
Canada	9.5	15.0

Source: Bank for International Settlements 1990

Since the crash, the emphasis has been on the relative stability not the target value of currencies.

Recently, banks have become less aggressive and more risk averse to maintain their capital adequacy ratios and the foreign exchange markets now respond less wildly to differences of opinion amongst the G7 leaders.

As the EC develops its own integrated single currency systems and moves towards a single central bank, there will be a lot less foreign exchange business within Europe. But the liberalization of eastern Europe will give rise to active zloty, forint and Romanian lei trading.

THE EUROPEAN MONETARY SYSTEM (EMS)

The EMS was established on 13 March 1979 and is run by the central banks of each member of the EC. The EMS consists of three complementary elements:

- the European Currency Unit (ECU)
- the Exchange Rate Mechanism (ERM)
- the European Monetary Co-operation Fund.

Greece and Portugal are currently outside the ERM but are part of the EMS so their currency contributes to the ECU and each has 20% of their foreign exchange reserves designated in ECUs to enable them to participate in the Co-operation Fund.

The overall objective of the EMS is to reduce the volatility of EC member currencies, through operation of the ERM and the Co-operation Fund. Britain is a member of the EMS, but not the ERM.

The Exchange Rate Mechanism (ERM)

The ERM is designed to limit the volatility of individual currencies. A central rate is determined in ECUs. The ECU is a composite currency made up of all the EC member currencies. The current weightings are reproduced below. The weighting is based on each country's relative GDP and share of EC trade. There is a re-weighting every five years. Realignment can occur at any time by agreement.

A member of the ERM had to ensure that its currency did not fluctuate more than 2.25% either side of the central rate. Since

	Weight in ECU	Currency amount equal to ECU on 28 November 1990
Deutsche Mark	30.1	2.05
French Franc	19.0	6.92
Pound Sterling	13.0	0.70
Dutch Guilder	9.4	2.31
Italian Lira	10.15	1540.67
Belgian Franc } Luxemborg Franc	7.6	42.35
Danish Krone	2.45	7.86
Irish Punt	1.10	0.76
Greek Drachma	0.8	179.00
Spanish Peseta	5.3	130.49
Portugese Escudo	0.8	179.00

September 1994, the band has widened to 15% for all remaining members (excluding Greece, Italy and the UK).

If day to day foreign exchange dealings push the value of a currency towards the lower limit, then the EMS central banks intervene by purchasing the weakest currency and selling the strongest. If this fails to maintain its value, the country with the weak currency has to raise interest rates, ask for a realignment, or suggest that others lower their interest rates. Conversely, if the upper limit is reached, the central banks sell the currency or the country cuts its interest rates, or asks for realignment at a higher value.

Membership of the ERM locks each country to one another, and inevitably their economic policies have to converge to some extent. Also, if the dominant currency in the ECU (the DM) is strengthening, the central rate itself strengthens, requiring that all other member currencies follow.

The European Monetary Union (EMU)

This is not a reality but is stage three of the Delors plan. The EMU requires that there be a common currency such as the ECU and will remove the need for foreign exchange transactions between member states. It is a long way off. Most European companies do not incorporate it into their long-term planning.

St Gobain, the French glass group, use the ECU to set internal transfer prices and have issued ECU bonds to raise loan finance.

But of 700 European companies only 44 had used the ECU for any purpose in 1989.

The ERM is designed to reduce the volatility of member currencies. This is of particular importance to small firms who wish to trade in the EC market. Currently, banks charge a hefty 1% on deals up to $10,000 but only 0.1% on large amounts. For deals within Europe, for the smaller firm, it is not cost effective to spread the risk by hedging – the currency losses are likely to be small and realignment should only occur infrequently.

The main currency problem and business risk is between the EMS currencies and the dollar. Here the swings are considerable and hedging essential in the short-term.

For the UK, when in the ERM the currency risk of sterling against EC currencies was reduced. This particularly benefited small to medium sized firms. For large firms with Treasury divisions, it made little difference.

But membership of the ERM considerably reduced the options the UK Government had to manage the economic cycle. Interest rates had to move to ensure they kept sterling within 6% either side of the central rate. It was not possible to devalue the currency to stimulate exports and economic growth in the two years before an election. Nor would it be possible to use a short appreciation (following higher interest rates) to operate an incomes policy on the UK tradable sector.

THE HARD ECU

The hard ECU was first mooted by the French in 1986 and subsequently refined by the British and outlined at the Madrid Conference in 1989. As a device it is intended to ease the movement by EC members towards stage three of the Delors plan, which envisages a single currency and a single European Reserve Bank.

The hard ECU will be a currency which initially will run in parallel with member states' currencies. The ECU would become legal tender at or around 1995 and be issued by the European Monetary Fund (EMF). The EMF would be owned by each country's reserve bank. Each central bank would be required to guarantee the exchange value of the EMF's holdings of its national currency against devaluation, following realignments.

The EMF would set interest rates on its own hard ECU liabilities (deposits) and influence hard ECU interest rates through buying and selling ECUs in open market operations. Excess holdings of any one national currency would be presented by the EMF to the central bank for payment in ECUs or other hard currency. There would be pre-set limits on how much national currency the EMF could hold.

Each country would still take its own decisions on monetary policy (within the constraints imposed by the ERM) and not collectively on the ECU via the EMF.

The ECU could become widely used as a means of settling transactions intra-Europe by companies and banks. It is unlikely to be used at the retail level in each country. The attraction to Corporates who may wish to borrow in ECUs is the low rate of interest (because of a commitment not to devalue by the EMF, the market would accept rates of interest probably below the lowest rate in any individual country).

This section is for specialist currency watchers

Each day (except Monday) the Financial Times publishes the chart reproduced in Table 9.2.

The first box, EMS European currency unit rates, shows the ECU central rates. These are set by the EC, and it is from these that the local currency value can be calculated. For example:

$$\frac{2.05586 \quad \text{D-Mark}}{0.696904 \quad \text{pound sterling}} = 2.95 \text{ DM to £1 Sterling}$$

The next column shows the currency amounts against the ECU on the previous day. These will change on a daily basis, because the ECU changes in value each day, because it consists of a basket of EC currencies.

The third column shows the deviation from the Central Rate.

The Spanish peseta is −2.34% from the Central Rate. This means that the peseta has STRENGTHENED against the Central Rate because the ECU has weakened. Sterling has WEAKENED against the Central Rate by 0.68%. (In effect the ECU has strengthened against the pound sterling).

The currencies are listed, strongest at the top, weakest at the

Table 9.2   EMS European currency unit rates

	ECU Central Rates	Currency Amounts Against ECU Nov. 28	Deviation from Central Rate	Spread v weakest Currency	Divergence Indicator
Spanish Pesatas	133.631	130.499	−2.34	3.10	41
D-Mark	2.05586	2.02080	−0.25	0.93	18
Dutch Guilder	2.31643	2.31346	−0.13	0.81	8
Belgian Franc	42.4032	42.3584	−0.11	0.79	7
Irish Punt	0.767417	0.768087	0.09	0.60	−3
Italian Lira	1538.24	1540.67	0.16	0.52	−6
Danish Krone	7.84195	7.86949	0.35	0.33	−15
French Franc	6.89509	6.92457	0.43	0.26	−22
Sterling	0.696904	0.701669	0.68	0.00	−13

bottom. The next column (4) shows the % spread against the weakest currency which will always be bottom of the list. The peseta is 3.10% stronger against sterling.

The final column is the 'divergence indicator' which shows that the peseta has moved 40% of the maximum allowable by ERM rates. Sterling has moved 13%. The peseta has strengthened, sterling has weakened.

What happens when there is a change in the exchange rate relative to other currencies?

Assume you are the export marketing manager for Jaguar cars. 50% of factory output is exported, the majority to the USA, the rest to the EC. Assume that Jaguar does no hedging against movements in the exchange rate. Assume that the factory price in sterling is increased each year in line with current year inflation. Assume no carriage insurance or freight costs.

Look at the figures in Table 9.3. The base year is 1977. In 1978, ex-factory prices rose by 9%, at the ruling average exchange rate this results in a 20% dollar price increase or if to Germany, a 3.4% D-Mark increase. This assumes our export manager passes the full effect of the exchange rate appreciation on. It is unlikely that he could raise his dollar price by 20% and maintain volumes – he therefore might decide to raise prices by US inflation (10%) thus cutting his margin per car.

As the car is manufactured in the UK and 80% of the components are sourced in the UK, our export manager would always prefer exchange rate depreciation to a strengthening, because as you can see from the table, a depreciation allows him to choose between price cuts in export markets (thus increasing share) and margin growth. Either way he wins.

A purchasing manager who imports materials from around the world would generally be in favour of exchange rate appreciation.

The exchange rate also has an impact on the reported earnings of UK subsidiaries. A strengthening domestic currency reduces the value of earnings in offshore companies. A devaluation increases the value of overseas earnings.

Going back to our Jaguar example; if the currency strengthens, then with a time lag pressure is increased for reductions in ex-factory prices. To maintain the manufacturing margin, productivity has to be raised; this normally means the same number of

Table 9.3   The impact of the exchange rate

Year	Average Rate Dollar/Sterling	UK Inflation	UK Product Price	US Product Price	US Price Change on Previous Year	DM Price Change on Previous Year
1977	1.74	16%	100	174	—	—
1978	1.92	9%	109	209	+20.0%	3.4
1979	2.12	13%	123	261	+24.0%	12.7
1980	2.32	18%	145	336	+29.0%	30.0
1981	2.00	12%	162	324	(3.5%)	20.0
1982	1.74	9%	176	307	(5.2%)	14.0
1983	1.51	5%	184	279	(10.0%)	(5.6)
1984	1.33	5%	193	256	(8.3%)	2.7
1985	1.29	6%	204	263	+2.7%	5.7
1986	1.40	4%	212	296	+12.3%	(13.0)
1987	1.64	4%	221	362	22.4%	(2.8)
1988	1.78	5%	232	413	+14.0%	13.0
1989	1.64	8%	250	410	(0.8%)	5.8
1990	1.76	9%	273	480	17.0%	5.0
1991	1.76	6%	289	508	6.0%	7.5
1992	1.76	4%	300	534	5.0%	(4.0)
1993	1.50	1.6%	305	457	(14.5%)	(8.3)

employees producing more or a smaller number of employees producing the same.

One of the reasons economists are in favour of a strengthening currency is that it acts as a downward pressure on domestic inflation because:

- Export margins are squeezed
- Export volumes are reduced
- Exporters drive up efficiency and cut costs
- The level of unemployment tends to increase
- Higher levels of unemployment reduce domestic spending and wage demands.

Exchange risk management

For any business cash is king. The role of corporate treasury is to manage corporate cash on behalf of the shareholders (the owners) and the business units (the users and generators). Any company with turnover in excess of £250 m (1992 prices) should have a dedicated corporate treasurer with or without an in-house team. BP's corporate treasury is larger than a small bank.

As 27% of the UK's GDP is derived from exports, a significant part of treasury activity is the managing of foreign exchange risk.

Sharp discontinuities in Government policies bring about large swings in the value of the currency; this can destroy the margin on what was planned to be a profitable export (or import) business.

HEDGING

Hedging is designed to reduce currency risk. The corporate treasurer must first decide the kind of exposure his company faces. There are two categories:

| 1 | Transactional exposure | This is the result of sales made in foreign currencies or borrowing in foreign currencies. Fluctuations in relative exchange rates cause changes in sterling cash terms, which have a direct impact on the Profit & Loss Account. |
| 2 | Translational exposure | This is the result of earnings in foreign currency which are given |

sterling equivalents for year end accounting purposes. A change in reported values can alter a company's net wealth and affect its borrowing capacity or dividend policy.

Now the Corporate Treasurer must decide on the appropriate hedging instrument.

- Forward contract — This locks the treasurer into exchanging cash at a predetermined rate at a fixed point in the future.
- Options — The treasurer places a bet on the future currency movements by paying a premium to a bank, for the delivery of currency at a future date and agreed price. If on the day the spot rate is below the agreed rate, the bank loses, the company gains, or vice versa.

What determines the exchange rate?

In a world of free flowing capital, the exchange rate of any currency is determined by the supply and demand for that currency at any given point in time.

Currency is purchased as an asset itself, to purchase paper assets such as equities, bonds and bills, or to purchase real assets such as land, buildings and equipment.

When purchasing a currency as an asset itself, there are two considerations. First, what will be the future value of the asset (in terms of other currencies) and second, what is the income stream (the rate of interest) from the asset. So the would-be purchaser is guessing future relative exchange rates and future relative interest rates.

Currency purchases in order to obtain paper assets are more complex because the yield on each item must be guessed and *then* the exchange rate risk applied. An equity yielding 10% will not be worth purchasing if the return after currency movements is, say, 2%.

The purchase of land, buildings and equipment is derived from some broader based demand, e.g. international expansion of manufacturing capacity, so the exchange rate may be less significant here.

In Table 9.1 you will have seen that currency flows across international exchanges are enormous – around 69 times larger than that required to finance transactions in real assets (as distinct from paper, i.e. equities, bonds and bills). So the majority of purchases of a currency are based on short-term considerations.

There are three interlocking items:

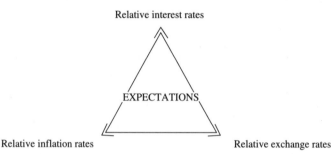

Relative interest rates

EXPECTATIONS

Relative inflation rates

Relative exchange rates

Each corner of the pyramid is determined by the other two in turn and movements in currency values are essentially caused by changes in expectations about future relativities. To a large extent, changed expectations are self-fulfilling. Hence a currency can often overshoot or undershoot its PPP value in the short run (see the beginning of this chapter).

Spot and forward exchange rates

An exchange rate is the price of foreign money at a particular point in time. The spot rate is the price of foreign money for immediate delivery. Descriptions of currency rates are often rather loose and can be misleading.

To guarantee clarity, identify the denominator as the currency which goes into the equation with a value of one. When an exchange rate appreciates, the denominator currency is getting stronger. When it shrinks the exchange rate is depreciating. The other currency weakens as the denominator strengthens.

So if $1 = Dm 2.00 becomes $1 = Dm 1.50 the denominator (the $) is shrinking, therefore the dollar has weakened against the German currency.

The forward exchange rate is used to determine a value today for a transaction that will take place at a given date in the future. The relationship between the spot rate and the forward rate is mathematical not behavioural; it depends on existing interest rate differentials.

Assume that a UK exporter of oil filters will be paid $1m in one month, on delivery of the filters. The exporter has most of his liabilities denominated in sterling. He wants to ensure a sterling return from the export to the USA. He will contact his bank who will guarantee a fixed amount of sterling in one month's time (our exporter is buying forward one month). The bank will borrow dollars for one month, sell them immediately for sterling; place the sterling in the money market to earn interest for a month. At the end of the month the bank gives the oil filter company sterling in exchange for dollars (at the predetermined rate) and uses the dollars to re-pay the dollar loan.

Forward rate agreements are not based on explicit expectations of exchange rate movements, but on spot rates and relative interest rates. For the bank in this example, the cost of the transaction is the interest paid on the loan in dollars less the interest received on the sterling deposit.

The dollars' forward rate would be higher than the spot rate if dollar interest rates were higher than sterling interest rates. Dollar forward would be at a premium.

On March 1st 1993 one month sterling interest rates were 6%; one month dollar interest rates were 3%. Therefore one month forward dollars were at a premium to spot sterling. If one month interest rates were identical in both countries, then the spot and forward rate would be the same. The premium expressed as an annual percentage is equal to the interest rate differential.

Rule of thumb

If sterling interest rates are below another currency's interest rates, sterling will trade at a discount to spot.

If sterling interest rates are above another currency's interest rates, sterling will trade at a premium to spot. The size of the discount or premium is equal to the interest rate differential.

Forward exchange rates and short-term capital movements

Short-Term Capital Movements (SCMs) come about as corporate treasurers, International banks and fund managers manage their liquid assets and switch between currencies. Bank deposits and government bonds near redemption are the main components of SCMs.

There are two main influences on SCMs; relative interest rates and expected exchange rates.

If a firm can borrow currencies at one rate and lend at a higher rate it will. If it can borrow at one rate in one currency and lend at a higher rate in another it might. SCMs tend to equalize international interest rates if exchange rates are fixed. If not, then the currency with high interest rates will strengthen and the currency with low interest rates will weaken. The forward market protects firms against risk. The covered interest differential drives SCMs. This is the difference between relative interest rates minus the forward value.

Forecasting interest rates

Short-term interest rates are difficult to forecast because movements are dominated by new information and expectations of new information and events.

To give an example, it was expected that short-term interest rates would fall on Budget Day in April 1987. Market makers expected $\frac{1}{2}\%$ reduction. They borrowed heavily in the overnight market (which pushed the overnight rate to 35%). They used the proceeds to purchase commercial and Treasury Bills at a yield of 9.5%. In the event, interest rates did fall $\frac{1}{2}\%$, and the price of commercial and Treasury Bills rose. Market makers sold their overnight holdings and used the capital gain to pay off their overnight loan plus interest. This had the impact of sharply increasing the overnight rate.

On Black Wednesday, September 16 1992 (the day the UK left the ERM) overnight rates rose to 100%. This is because the Bank of England was intervening in the foreign exchange market purchasing sterling and selling D-marks. Thus there was a severe shortage of sterling deposits in the market and the clearing banks bid up overnight interest rates for cash to balance their books.

These events are in the main unpredictable over the medium

term (three months to one year). Over the longer term (one to five years) guesses can be made.

We start with the key, long run forces which affect domestic interest rates.

The domestic interest rate should equal the foreign interest rate plus the expected depreciation in the domestic currency, plus a risk premium.

So what determines long run forecasts?

1   The monetary stance of the Federal Reserve and the Bundes bank.
2   Expected, relative inflation rates.
3   The relative attractiveness of the domestic economy (risk premium); factors here are:
    (a)   perception of sound government policies
    (b)   productivity
    (c)   inward net investment
    (d)   the price of north sea oil.

A basic tenet of market behaviour is buy on the rise, sell at the top and during the fall. This 'speculative' behaviour is common in the foreign exchange market.

A government may change relative interest rates, instigating an increase in demand for its currency. The price begins to rise and as a result so does the quantity demanded. An upward price spiral begins and people purchase the currency, precisely because its price is rising.

At some point 'based on fundamentals' the players decide the top has been reached and price begins to collapse as people sell something before its price falls. Quantity supplied exceeds demand, and the price collapses.

This is a common feature of foreign exchange markets, particularly since 1979 when most major countries began dismantling foreign exchange controls.

What is the 'correct' value for a country's currency?

Most economists distinguish between the market value (which is determined by supply and demand at a particular point in time) and the 'fair' value. The fair value is the value of the exchange rate which equalizes the prices of tradable goods in the UK and overseas in terms of a common currency. This is known as the purchasing power parity exchange rate. For the UK, recognition of where we do international tradable business is important. The trade weighted index would reflect sterling's value against other European currencies and the US dollar. So the correct value for the currency would be the market value = the purchasing power parity value of the trade weighted index.

The behaviour of the real exchange rate

Figure 9.1 shows the deviation of sterling's trade weighted index from its estimated purchasing power parity level. A positive deviation indicates sterling overvaluation, a negative deviation undervaluation.

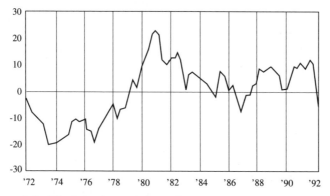

Figure 9.1 The behaviour of the real exchange rate
Source: T Congdon, Gerrard & National Economic Review Nov. '92

Figure 9.1 also shows that throughout most of the eighties sterling was overvalued; and throughout most of the seventies it was undervalued.

The link between the exchange rate, the level of economic activity and the inflation rate

As we have already discussed, a devaluation improves exporters' profit margins and their price competitiveness.

As exports represent about 27% of GDP, a devaluation has considerable, positive multiplier effects. Thus a devaluation is expansionary. If the economy has limited spare capacity, bottle-necks appear very quickly and in particular markets prices move upwards. These are passed on in the form of higher ex-factory gate prices, and requires further devaluation to maintain international price competitiveness. In short, devaluation is expansionary, economic activity increases and, with time lags, bottlenecks appear, pushing up prices.

Because of the multiplier effect, an increase in business activity in the tradable export sector spreads to the domestic non-tradable sector (e.g. services) and if bottlenecks appear in this sector prices rise too.

In the context of the UK there is a further consideration, the wage bargaining process. A devaluation improves earnings in the tradable sector, in particular skilled and semi-skilled employees enjoying creative and bonus payments. The index of average earnings shows sharp increases.

The non-tradable service sectors then experience wage claims to maintain differentials. Productivity increases are difficult to achieve, so the wage awards are not self-funding and service firms raise their prices. As a consequence the Retail Price Index moves upwards and there is wage inflation.

Under these circumstances it is argued that devaluation causes inflation. In the seventies, Government tried to prevent the inflationary impact by means of wage and price controls. In the early eighties Government either knowingly or unknowingly achieved an overvaluation which caused a substantial reduction in the Retail Price Index. This was achieved by creating substantial excess capacity in the UK tradable sector and surplus skilled and semi-skilled labour.

As unemployment rose steadily from 1.6 million to 3 million, so trades union membership fell and the ability to maintain wage differentials was weakened. Thus throughout the economy wage pressure was reduced by excess capacity. Where sharp increases in wages were given, in the majority of cases these were self-funding with little or no impact on final selling prices.

It can be argued that a devaluation at near full employment is inflationary. That a devaluation with high unemployment is expansionary first, inflationary second, and that one of the best ways of keeping retail price increases low is to run a domestic monetary policy which overvalues the currency, but simultaneously creates excess capacity. This is summarized in Figures 9.2 and 9.3.

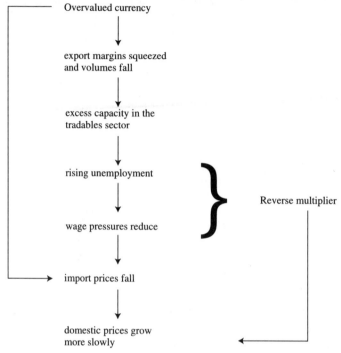

Figure 9.2 The effect of an overvalued currency

CHAPTER SUMMARY

- Exchange rates are the price of one country's currency in terms of another. There are three theories of exchange rate determination; the Purchasing Power Parity, the Monetary and the Asset Market. The current popular view is a mixture.
- A currency can undershoot or overshoot its purchasing power parity, particularly if Government allows large swings in the domestic money supply.
- The Foreign Exchange market in the UK, Japan, USA and Germany trades currency many times the value of trade.
- The Exchange Rate Mechanism within the European Monetary System is designed to minimize exchange rate fluctuations between market currencies.

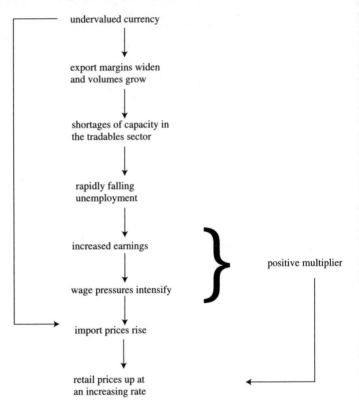

Figure 9.3   The effect of an undervalued currency

- Managing exchange risk is an important role for corporate treasurers using hedging devices.
- The relative value of a currency can have a significant impact on domestic economic activity via exporters profit margins.

10 *Forecasting the economy*

FORECASTING THE ECONOMY

Economic activity is the result of people acting in a particular way. Forecasting is guessing how people will act in the future, based on partial knowledge of how they have acted in the past. Because people are inconsistent their past behaviour is only a guide to their future behaviour. When forecasting there are two main rules of thumb. The first is never to predict the event and the timing simultaneously because one of them is bound to be wrong. The second is to be broadly right rather than precisely wrong.

In this chapter we will discuss some of the approaches to forecasting and the issues arising, finishing with the back of the envelope approach.

There is in the UK a variety of forecasting groups. The largest is the Government's own forecasting unit in the Treasury, the smallest is a team run by Tim Congdon at Lombard Street Research Ltd. Since the mid-eighties the Congdon team have been consistently more accurate than the Treasury. It could be luck, but it is more likely to be based on a superior understanding of how the economy actually works. The differences in thinking and analysis are grouped into schools of macro economic thought. Each forecasting group bases its view of the future on the past and according to assumptions on how the economy works. It is important to know which school of economic thinking the forecaster belongs to, to understand the basis of their forecast and the judgements they make.

The Monetarist

The monetarist school assumes that money drives economic activity. The Chicago School under Milton Friedman has shown that there is an econometric relationship between money and economic activity. In the UK there are some keen supporters of the monetarist view that a single monetary variable (for example, the amount of cash in issue) can explain future activity.

Professor Minford of Liverpool University believes M0 (cash in issue plus bankers deposits at the central bank) is the best indicator; Sir Alan Walters broadens to M1 (cash plus non-interest bearing current accounts) – a view shared by Professor Gordon Pepper of Midland Montague and more broadly by an ex-Treasury economist now at UBS Phillips and Drew, Mr Bill Martin, who prefers M2 (cash plus sterling retail deposits in banks and building societies and national savings). The question mark in the box above describes the inadequacy of this approach, which essentially says the relationship between money and activity is because it is. There is a lack of explanation as to why money drives activity; what is known in the trade as the 'transmission mechanism'.

At Lombard Street Research Ltd., Tim Congdon has refined work done by himself, Peter Warburton and Paul Turnbull when they were a team at L. Messel and Co., a City firm of stockbrokers (now part of Lehmans). This work has refined substantially the simple monetarist view that money drives activity, by concentrating on the transmission mechanism. In doing so, Congdon concentrates on behaviour and what drives it. He has developed the concept of monetary equilibrium to explain how behaviour changes when money supply changes.

The Lombard Street research approach

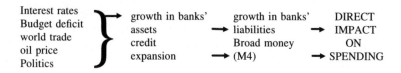

Interest rates, Budget deficit, world trade, oil price, Politics } → growth in banks' assets credit expansion → growth in banks' liabilities Broad money (M4) → DIRECT IMPACT ON SPENDING

It is worth making the effort to understand this concept; it will probably underpin most macro economic analysis in the late nineties.

Equilibrium is a point in time when relationships in the system are unchanged. In a market economy individuals make purchase decisions on the basis of relative prices (these, in relation to the performance of each good or service, give each of us the subjective notion of 'value for money'). If relative prices change, assessments of value for money and behaviour (i.e. purchase decisions) change. A change in relative prices with a time lag produces changes in volumes of goods and services, so if the price of beer rises through time relative to the price of wine, then less beer and more wine is purchased (exactly as has happened in the eighties in the UK).

Congdon argues that money is a good just like beer, wine, houses and cars. Money has a price (the rate of interest). The decision to hold money or exchange it for goods and services depends on relative prices (i.e. the rate of interest compared to the rate of return on other goods and services.)

If the rate of return on bank deposits goes up relative to other assets, then people will hold more bank deposits (in relation to their income). If the rate of return on bank deposits goes down, people will switch from bank deposits to goods and services.

This over-simplifies human behaviour and there are more influences which will be discussed later in this chapter, but in essence the approach says that at given relative prices, monetary equilibrium is where the demand for money (i.e. amount of notes, coin, and bank deposits) is equal to the supply of money (the amount of notes, coins and bank deposits in existence). In disequilibrium, people change their behaviour in order to restore equilibrium.

For the purpose of analysis it has to be assumed that there are points in time when monetary equilibrium exists, and the demand for money is matched with the supply of money at a given rate of interest and set of relative prices in the economy as a whole.

If we accept the concept of monetary equilibrium, then for forecasting purposes the key is to understand how people behave under conditions of disequilibrium and how in their pursuit of equilibrium, the real economy is affected.

Take a simple example. The price of beer increases. More money is needed than before to achieve identical physiological effects. The pub only takes cash (notes and coin). Individuals draw more cash from their bank to finance their night out in the pub. They transfer from a current account to notes and coin. If there is widespread demand for more notes and coin, it is made available by the central bank on demand from the clearing banks.

The real economy is not affected; but the amount of notes and coin in existence increases. Indeed, there will be a close fit between the amount of notes and coin (MO) and Nominal GDP (which there is). But this does not tell us that MO drives Nominal GDP, rather it suggests that when an individual experiences monetary disequilibrium, a set of financial transactions restore it and, as a consequence, narrow money responds and because the banking system is efficient, the amount of narrow money people would wish to hold is equal to the amount in existence at almost every point in time. In short, narrow money is usually in equilibrium.

Broad money is the total of all bank deposits in the economy. The decision by one person in the system to increase his holdings of bank deposits, reduces another's and unless bank credit increases, the total amount of deposits remain unchanged. However, if people believe their holdings of broad money are too large as a whole, they will attempt to reduce them by purchasing goods and services thereby causing a change in nominal GDP. Thus broad money disequilibrium can bring about significant changes in the level of economic activity as individuals try to restore equilibrium. It's a zero sum game. As individual A spends his bank deposit, individual B who supplies the good or services gains a new deposit. The total amount of deposits is unchanged. One individual can only reduce his deposits if others are induced to increase theirs by the same amount.

This is the key. As individuals attempt to reduce their holdings of broad money, the level of economic activity increases. This activity may be larger volumes at existing prices or the same volumes at higher prices, or any combination in between. It depends on the supply side. Expenditure decisions will continue to change until individuals have restored their equilibrium, where their desire for broad money is matched by their holding of it. This explains how the economy adjusts to changes in broad money, and is the basic plank of the Lombard Street Research approach.

Assume that rising unemployment is increasing the unpopularity of a Government with a small majority (say 18 seats). The Bank of England is instructed to lower interest rates by the Chancellor. At lower interest rates, borrowing becomes more attractive because there will be a wide range of assets (particularly housing, commercial property and land) where the expected return will exceed the cost of borrowed funds. People borrow and spend on these assets. Broad money increases as a consequence and other people find their holdings of money excessive, so they look for things to purchase: they purchase cars, clothes, hi-fi, shares, insurance policies, holidays, computers, works of art, lawn-mowers, management courses and books on economics. As the new deposits change hands, there is a sense that the economy is recovering. New incomes are generated as individuals try to eliminate their excess holding of broad money. In due course asset prices begin to rise and, with the exception of land, people increase the supply of assets – more cars are made, more offices built and more books published. There is a time lag but eventually excess holdings are eliminated by a sharp rise in the prices of assets: the Government raises interest rates and credit growth slows; thus with a time lag, asset prices fall.

The Lombard Street Research Group thus believe that growth in bank credit leads to excess money holdings (monetary disequilibrium) which in turn causes a change in spending as people try to restore their monetary equilibrium. For forecasting purposes, the Group have produced a model which relies on around fifty equations. The key relationships and assumptions are as follows:

1 Interest rates are determined by the central bank.
2 The quantity of money is determined by the level of banks' assets, and its rate of growth by the growth rate of bank credit.
3 The desired stock of credit is inversely related to interest rates.

4 The quantity of narrow money (i.e. notes, coin, and non-interest bearing deposits) has no impact on spending behaviour, but is instead determined by the amount of spending in the economy.

5 The quantity of broad money has important effects on the economy only when its supply exceeds the demand to hold it, i.e. there is monetary disequilibrium.

6 The personal sector rarely suffers from disequilibrium; it is found mostly in corporate and non-bank financial sectors. It is indicated by balance sheet positions and has an impact on a range of asset prices. In particular,

- share prices
- house prices
- the exchange rate
- non-residential property prices
- antiques
- ships
- aircraft
- footballers
- horses etc.

7 If the market price of an asset differs from its economic value (estimated from the discounted present value of the future profits stream) and its replacement cost, then either investment occurs (market price is higher) or disinvestment occurs (market price is lower).

Fluctuations in private sector spending on investment goods and consumer durables can be largely explained by financial events. The fluctuations usually reflect monetary disequilibrium.

8 Fluctuations in investment drive the business cycle; variations in the inflation rate reflect pressures in the goods and labour markets, but are ultimately determined by monetary policy.

The standard Keynesian model

This model assumes that the level of spending is determined by a number of exogenous variables (e.g. tax rates, world trade and interest rates). The relative importance of each is determined by statistical tests on historic data. The UK Treasury has the largest of these models.

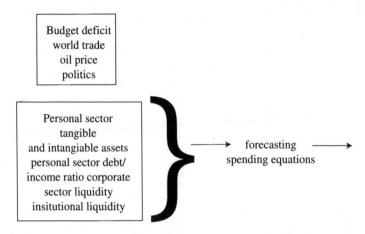

Figure 10.1 Summary of the Lombard Street Ltd forecasting approach

There are 300 simultaneous equations (in 1977 there were 500) which show, for example, that consumer spending is related to past consumer spending, current and past income and wealth and real interest rates. Around twenty economists work on the model full time. The equations are estimated by using increasingly sophisticated mathematical techniques, which can explain history accurately and produce good forecasts if the future is almost identical to the past. There are problems with the statistics used – in 1988 estimates of GDP for the UK varied by 10%. When behaviour changes history is of limited help, e.g. after financial deregulation in the mid-eighties.

Exogenous variables (influences on the system not determined by the system itself) are guessed at, so unexpected policy changes can ruin the accuracy of a forecast. The equations are necessarily simplifications of life and therefore there is usually a gap between what the model thinks should have happened and the actual event. This gap is closed by the use of 'add factors' which the economist applies to get a good fit. The choice of add factor is a question of judgement. Treasury economists are in general an unworldly bunch and risk averse, so they are conservative in their assessment of changes in the economy. Recessions are always sharper and deeper than they expect and recovery always stronger.

The Chancellor can amend any forecast and publish them in accordance with his own views. Inevitably, the economists are aware of the Chancellor's ideological preferences and will shade their view to fit. Some have argued that there is too much shading and insufficient rigour in the process, particularly since a mass exodus of Treasury economists in the mid-eighties to better paid City jobs; but the City firms have not been markedly better in their forecasts, with the possible exception of Lombard Street Research Ltd. who recognized much earlier than most the way in which financial deregulation changed the behaviour of key players in the system.

A problem for all forecasters is an exogenous shock like an oil price hike. The definition of a shock is that it cannot be forecast and it renders all forecasts wrong. Some key shocks in the world have been changes in oil prices in 1973, 1979, 1986 (collapse) 1990 (Kuwait). For the UK, joining the ERM in Sept 1990 and departing in Sept 1992 are particular shocks.

Figure 10.2   The Keynesian forecasting approach

BACK OF THE ENVELOPE FORECASTING

An experienced economist is like an experienced meteorologist; both look at past patterns, sense the present and use their judgement (based on history) to take a view on, or make a forecast of, the future. Both are trained to handle large quantities of data, they understand some of the theories of the behaviour of the thing they are forecasting, and they are often wrong. A country shepherd will usually be correct in his weather forecast because he has experienced so much of it during his life.

Anyone who has run a business for say twenty years, for similar reasons is usually fairly accurate on the economy. This section is designed for people in business who would like to find out why their forecasts have been right (or wrong) in the past; and those who would like to start from first principles.

First, define the business you are in – this is crucial; does the business supply a product or service, is it essential for the consumer, or for another business, or is it a fashion item or nice to have but not essential? Where in the economic chain does the business fit? Is it a raw material business, or distribution, or retail business? What are the key drivers of its volumes? Does the business supply a consumer product or a capital product, does the customer buy regularly or periodically?

To give examples – food is regularly purchased; but televisions are not. Food is the classic consumption product; televisions are the classic consumer durable; once purchased, they provide a stream of benefits to the purchaser well beyond the purchase date. Is the business a business-to-business activity, for example, office stationery, (a consumption product) or filing cabinets (a durable product).

Before a sales forecast can be finalized, a forecast of overall economic activity has to be made; in short, a view on where the economy is and where it is headed has to be taken. We need to be able to forecast the stages of the business cycle and discover the current position. Back to the chart first seen in Chapter 4 and reproduced below in figure 10.3

Stage A: the recovery

After a period (lasting two years) of declining or flat retail sales (measured on an annual percentage change basis) the consumer begins to spend again. This is for a number of reasons; the most significant is that for two years or more, consumers have delayed their purchase decisions by making their existing stock of goods last longer. Shoes are repaired not replaced, suits are made to last longer, carpets are cleaned not replaced, the washing machine is repaired not replaced, the car is got through the MOT by the garage with the warning that next year it will be more difficult (i.e. more expensive) to achieve. But there comes a time when clothes, carpets, cars and washing machines are no longer serviceable and have to be replaced. The consumer has the money because

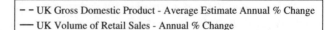

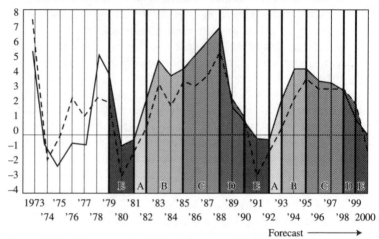

Figure 10.3 The stages of the cycle

interest rates have fallen (mortgage payments are lower thus increasing discretionary income), and fear of unemployment has caused increased saving. Hard pressed retailers are offering interest free credit, discounts and other attractive promotions. Replacement demand becomes widespread. This unexpected (by retailers and manufacturers) increase in volume is met by stock reduction, but after about six months manufacturing output begins to increase and stage B of the recovery begins.

Key indicators of stage A are:

1 Retail sales volumes expressed as a percentage increase on the same period 12 months earlier, are higher than expected.
2 Short term interest rates are falling.
3 Unemployment, month on month, continues to increase.
4 An increase in the number of new houses started.
5 FT 500 share index increases, and dividend yield tends to fall.
6 Narrow money M0 increases at a rate faster than previous five years.
7 Broad money M4 increases.
8 Industrial production stagnant.

9 Retail prices growing slowly, say 2% a year, but some prices falling, particularly raw material prices.

10 Earnings growth at record lows.

The Key Indicators of stage B are:

1 Retail sales volumes up at an increasing rate.
2 Short-term interest rates stop falling.
3 Unemployment stops rising, then begins to fall.
4 Number of houses built continues to grow.
5 FT 500 share index rate of increase shows.
6 M0 continues to grow.
7 Rate of increase in Broad money M4 quickens.
8 Industrial production ahead of retail sales growth.
9 Sharp increases in notified vacancies.
10 Retail prices growing slowly, but raw material prices now increasing.
11 Earnings boosted by overtime working.

The system now moves on to stage C

Around three years after the initial increase in retail sales (Stage A) manufacturing businesses begin to add capacity in the form of new buildings, equipment, heavy vehicles and new employees. There is a surge in investment spending, which boosts incomes still further.

This is Stage C and lasts about two to four years and causes the economy to overheat: prices in general are rising more rapidly than in the past five years, the balance of payments deficit on current account widens.

The Government takes action: interest rates are raised, discretionary income is squeezed, confidence falters and retail sales go negative.

The key indicators of stage C are:

1 Retail Sales volumes growing at 3% to 4% per annum.
2 Short-term interest rates moving upwards.
3 Unemployment continues to fall.
4 Number of new houses started continues to grow but at a slower rate.
5 FT 500 share index still rising, but erratically.

6 Narrow and broad money continue to grow, but rate of growth in M4 is higher than M0.
7 Industrial production rate of growth in line with retail sales.
8 Continuing growth in number of declared vacancies: skills shortages reported in key sectors.
9 Retail prices begin to inch upwards.
10 Earnings above retail prices by around 3%.

Stage D

This stage lasts about two to four years. Everyone in the system is conserving cash and velocity is falling sharply. Broad money growth slows dramatically; corporate balance sheets are strained and unemployment begins to rise, further dampening consumer spending and raising the savings ratio.

The key indicators of stage D are:

1 Rate of growth in retail sales slows.
2 Short-term interest rates continue to increase (and are around 4% above the inflation rate as measured by RPI).
3 Unemployment continues to fall but at a much slower rate.
4 House building stalls.
5 FT share index falls.
6 M0 continues to grow.
7 M4 continues to grow.
8 Industrial production slightly higher than the now lower than expected retail sales.
9 Retail prices continue to grow.
10 Earnings growth slows as hours worked as overtime falls quickly.

Stage E

Stage E is characterized by sharp falls in industrial production; it falls by more than the reduction in the retail sales due to destocking as companies put cash before profit. Retail sales are negative for up to two years. Asset prices stop rising and may even fall. Unemployment begins to rise. There is a general sense of gloom, as businesses run for cash and cut any expenditure which is considered to be peripheral.

The Key indicators of stage E are:

1 Retail sales negative.
2 Short-term interest rates increase, then fall sharply.
3 Unemployment begins to increase; slowly at first, then rapidly.
4 House building falls.
5 FT share index begins to increase as interest rates come down.
6 M0 growing very slowly.
7 M4 growing very slowly in nominal terms (but could be falling in real terms).
8 Industrial production falling (rate of decrease is higher than retail sales).
9 Retail prices growing very slowly or not at all.
10 Earnings growth at very low levels.

The schematic diagram in Figure 10.4 shows the behaviour of three of the variables discussed. The business cycle can be shorter than the seven years shown in the diagram. Not all economies go through stages E and A. In fact the Asian Tigers, South Korea, Thailand, Singapore, Indonesia and until recently, Japan, do not experience negative growth in investment spending; they are known as investment led economies because they are starting from a low invested base. They only experience stages C and D.

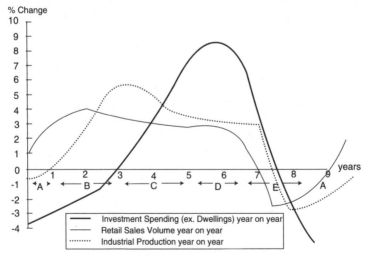

Figure 10.4 Schematic representation of the business cycle

Spotting turning points: the cyclical indicators

When doing a sales forecast, there is a need to monitor the sales environment. Will incomes continue to grow at the same rate? Will customers' confidence be maintained? If we expect growth in sales, at what rate? The vast majority of sales forecasts are backcasts – the forecaster projects forward previously established trends. The key is to be able to anticipate turning points; the cyclical indicators published monthly in Economic Trends by the Central Statistical Office (CSO) provide an insight to future turning points.

The CSO has monitored a variety of time series since the war. Some of these have shown that a relatively constant relationship exists between the movement of different economic variables over time. So although no single economic series exhibits a constant pattern of movement over time, it is often possible to find a series of economic variables which are related to each other and find that some lead the others. The leading series can be used to forecast change in the others.

The indicators are reproduced in Table 10.1 and Figure 10.5. Some points to note:

1   The indicators give warning of *turning points* not size of expansion or contraction.
2   The indicators are of growth cycles, which in turn are cyclical movements in the deviation from a long run trend.
3   An expansion phase occurs when the rate of growth in the indicator is above the long run trend.
4   Special economic and climatic factors are discounted.

The overall state of the economy, particularly its rate of growth, will determine the rate at which a product will pass through its life cycle. All other things assumed equal. Marketing efforts may well determine market share, but the economy as a whole will determine the size of the market and its rate of growth.

Table 10.1 The cyclical indicators

| Average −12 months | | NOW +3-6 MONTHS | |
| | | Average | Average +12 months |
Lagging	*Coincident*	*Shorter leading*	*Longer leading*
Investment in plant and machinery	GDP	Gross trading profits industrial and commercial companies	New housing starts
Notified vacancies	Volume of retail sales	New retail credit New car registrations	3 month inter-bank interest rate
Unemployment (excluding adult students and school leavers)	Index of manufacturing output	Bankruptcies	Net acquisition of financial assets by industrial and commercial companies
Orders in hand, engineering sector	CBI survey actual level of stocks. CBI survey of firms working at capacity	CBI survey expected level of stocks	Financial Times 500 share index

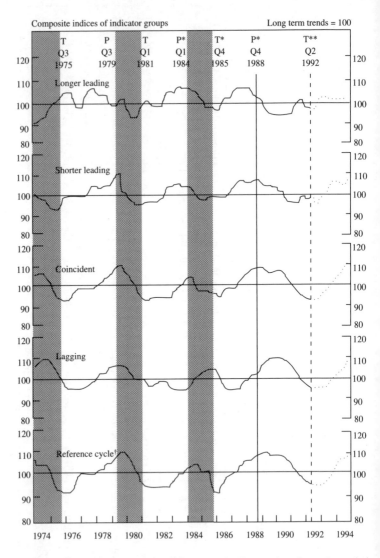

Composite indices of indicator groups   Long term trends = 100

| T Q3 1975 | P Q3 1979 | T Q1 1981 | P* Q1 1984 | T* Q4 1985 | P* Q4 1988 | T** Q2 1992 |

Figure 10.5 The cyclical indicators

- - - Subject to revision due to trend re-estimation
····· Based on incomplete data
† Deviation of gross domestic product at constant factor cost (strike adjusted) from its long term trend value

* These turning points are less marked than previous peaks and troughs
** Provisional date

APPENDIX 10.A

Other sources of data

Every Friday the Chancellor is given a report detailing what has happened in the economy over the previous fortnight and some of the following is included.

Retail sales

30 of Britain's largest stores which account for half the turnover in the retail sector add up their revenues each week. By the following Tuesday each company knows the sales for the group as a whole. The Chancellor knows too, but the general public has to wait for the 'official' figures for retail sales.

Clothing and footwear sales

Six companies – House of Fraser, Marks & Spencers, Storehouse, Burton, Sears and John Lewis – collaborate and supply weekly data for about 10% of retail sales. Price Waterhouse collates the data which is sent to the Treasury. John Lewis is the only retailer which publishes its sales on a weekly basis.

Money supply

A group of 90 large banks gives information to the Bank of England about its lending patterns each week. The data is available on the following Wednesday to the Treasury but not the public.

Building societies also supply weekly lending figures to the Building Societies Commission, the industry watchdog. The Treasury, but not the public, gets these figures.

The big building societies also supply weekly data on house sales.

Air transport

British Airways and BAA produce monthly data on passenger and aircraft movements. But the split by route is kept secret. British Airways knows each day how many passengers have flown, but keep this secret.

Car registrations

DVLA in Swansea supplies data to the Society of Motor Manufacturers and Traders, who publish the figures on the fourth working day of the following month.

Recruitment

MSC monitors job advertisements in newspapers to measure demand for senior managers in industry and public services. The MSC index is published once a quarter.

Trade

The CSO figures on visible trade are published at least six weeks out of date.

P & O publishes figures on its cargoes between UK and continental Europe.

Industry

Two good indicators are semiconductor production and sales and plastic sheeting.

The Electronic Component Industry Federation publishes monthly figures for semiconductors. There are no published figures for plastic sheeting.

International telephone calls

BT produces internal figures for the volume of calls. These are not made public; but are a good indicator of activity.

CHAPTER SUMMARY

- Economic forecasting is just like weather forecasting. Historical patterns are projected for the future, but because past behaviour is only a guide to future behaviour, forecasts are always wrong.
- There are different schools of thought which emphasize different economic variables as the key drivers of activity.
- The styles of the economic cycle can be spotted from data published each week at the back of the Economist.
- The Central Statistical Office produces its own cyclical indicators which are quite good for spotting turning points.

Conclusion and
self-assessment test

Economics is a behavioural science. It is impossible to run a controlled experiment and thereby establish whether laws exist. There are no laws; but there are general tendencies. History does repeat itself, not exactly, but a pattern can be discerned.

I hope that you, reader, have been made aware of the general tendencies and can use this knowledge to reduce business and personal risk (or to take a gamble on the next upswing!)

We humans are always adapting to our environment; as a consequence each decision we take has an impact on others, however small. Everything is influencing everything else; the system is continually flexing, adapting and moving. Our behaviour is key.

It is an exciting area for study and although it is necessary to assume all other things being equal to pinpoint key elements of the system, the attraction is that things never are equal. Change is continuous; and it is change which causes all the emotion and excitement in our daily lives. The pace seems to be quickening. The future promises even more excitement. No one wants stability; Governments cannot deliver it.

The essence of capitalism is risk and as individuals take risks, in general, the well-being of all is improved.

I look forward to the next boom and I hope you'll be prepared for the inevitable bust. This assumes that our behaviour is fundamentally unchanged. I think this is a reasonable assumption to make. Do you?

SELF-ASSESSMENT TEST

This section is designed to test your understanding of the economy. The answers are at the back of the book. If you get an answer wrong, re-read the chapter. Some of the questions are necessarily over-simplistic, and the nature of the subject is such that you would want to say "yes but. . . ."!

Questions

1. What is GDP?
2. What is GNP?
3. If you grow your own vegetables, and consume them, does this contribute to the GDP or the GNP?
4. What is the difference between Nominal GDP and Real GDP?
5. Consider the two countries below. The figures are average growth rates over the last ten years, from the same base.

	A	B
Nominal GDP	10%	8%
Retail Prices	9%	5%

Which country is growing faster, in real terms?

6. If people plan to save more than companies plan to invest, all other things being equal, what will happen to the rate of growth in real GDP?
7. What is meant by the term 'the paradox of thrift'?
8. What do you understand by the term 'multiplier effect'?
9. If people save more all other things being equal, will the level of economic activity:
   (a) fall by the amount saved
   (b) fall by an amount greater than the savings
   (c) stay the same
   (d) expand
   (e) expand by an amount greater than the savings
10. If people decide to save £100 or 10% of their disposable income and it is immediately invested by companies, in theory how much new income will be created?
11. What is the difference between cash and PLC money?

12. The amount of cash in the UK economy has been falling steadily as a proportion of nominal GDP, since 1924. Why?
13. What has happened to velocity over the same period?
14. What is PLC money?
15. If a stand alone bank has customers, who on average require 10% of their deposits in cash and who have £100 in the bank, how much credit can a bank create?
16. What are the limits to credit creation?
17. In the UK is it liquidity or capital which limits the growth of a bank's balance sheet?
18. If a bank retains £1 Billion of profits by how much in principle could it increase its balance sheet?
    (a) 10 times
    (b) 15 times
    (c) 8 times
    (d) 12.5 times.

19. What, in the main, drives a bank's willingness to lend to a private individual?
20. What is the difference between the short run rate of interest and the long run rate of interest?
21. If the Central Bank decides to tighten monetary policy how would it do it?
22. What would be the effect on long run interest rates?
23. Explain the difference between yield and rate of return.
24. If the chairman of a UK public company tells shareholders his overall aim is to increase shareholder value, what does he mean?
25. What is the main difference between a gilt edged security and a treasury bill?
26. If M4 is growing by 10%, velocity is growing by 1%, the volume of transactions by 6%, what will be the rate of change in prices?
    (a) 10%
    (b) 3%
    (c) 16%
    (d) 5%.

27. If velocity increased to 4%, all other things being the same, what would the rate of change in prices be?
    (a) 20%
    (b) 8%

(c) 6%

(d) 12%

28. The table below shows basic indicators for a number of Eastern European countries.

	A	B	C	D	E	F	G
Population	286	9	15	16	10	38	23
GDP $ Bn	1590	50	118	155	68	207	94
GDP $ per capita	5552	563	7603	9361	6491	545	411
Cars per 1000	50	127	182	206	153	74	11
Telephones per 1000	124	248	246	233	152	122	111

Can you match each letter with a country from the following list?

- Russia
- Romania
- Bulgaria
- Czechoslovakia (combined)
- East Germany
- Poland
- Hungary

Which country, based on the limited information available, is the most attractive?

Answers

1. GDP is an estimate of the value of final sales of goods and services in the economy with the value of imports subtracted.
2. GNP is GDP, with a further adjustment. The income from overseas assets owned by UK residents is added, the income paid to overseas residents from UK assets is subtracted.
3. GDP/GNP is an estimate of final *sales*.
   Goods and services not sold are excluded, therefore the vegetables are not included.
4. Nominal GDP is the value of final sales measured at market prices. Real GDP is obtained by adjusting nominal for changes in the average level of prices, using the GDP deflater.
5. Country B; its real GDP is growing by 8% minus 5% = 3%.
6. The rate of growth in real GDP will slow and possibly GDP could contract, as the system adjusts to ensure savings equal investment.

7. The paradox of thrift was first pointed out by John Maynard Keynes in 1927. He explained how households, by increasing their rate of saving (to improve their future prospects) were actually reducing their incomes via the multiplier effect. Keynes showed that rising unemployment was due to lack of effective demand, and it could be cured by getting people to reduce their savings or by Government running a budget deficit, financed by household savings.

8. The multiplier effect is a fundamental activity in a market economy. It shows that one man's income is another man's expenditure. An increase in one will increase the other; an increase in spending will cause an increase in output a number of times larger than the original amount.

9. (b) Fall by an amount greater than the savings. This is due to the multiplier.

10. The multiplier is $\dfrac{1}{\text{savings ratio}} = \dfrac{1}{10} = 10$

So £100 of new investment will generate 10 x 100 = £1000 of new incomes IN THEORY!

11. Cash is legal tender – coins and notes issued by the Royal Mint and Bank of England respectively. It is tangible, you can feel it, like it, touch it. It is perfectly liquid: you can *always* exchange it for a good or service.

    PLC money is the bulk of the liabilities of the commercial banking system. It is intangible and consists of entries in ledgers and on computer files. It is the dominant component of M4. It expands as a result of increase in bank lending either to the public or direct to the Government. PLC money is shifted from account to account by use of cheque, switch or direct debit instructions.

12. The increasing issue of credit transfer as a means of payment. Since 1924, there has been a steady reduction in the number of employers who pay their employees cash. Simultaneously there has been an increase in the percentage of the population with a bank or building society account, and the use of cheques to settle debt.

    Banks do try to get their customers to use non-cash payment systems. These are much easier to computerize and generally reduce the chance of errors or losses. The widespread use of Access, Visa and Switch as a cash substitute.

13. The velocity of M0 (= cash) has risen steadily as its use has declined.

$$\text{Velocity} = \frac{\text{nominal GDP}}{\text{notes \& coin in circulation}}$$

14. PLC money is a clearing bank's liability. It comes into existence when a bank lends to a customer or the Government. The basic rule is; every loan creates a deposit.

15. The bank has enough cash (liquidity) to support total liabilities of £1000. The bank can create £900 of advances and hence £900 of liabilities, in addition to the £100 of liabilities and cash it starts with.

16. There are many. The more significant is the 8% capital ratio which banks must conform to. For every £1 of shareholders' funds plus long-term debt, a bank can create £12.50 of liabilities. It is unlikely that a bank would run to the limit.

17. It is capital. Liquidity is not a problem. The Bank of England as lender of last resort will always let the banking system have the liquidity it needs.

18. (d) 12.5 times

19. Banking is a risk business. Lending to an individual will depend on:
    (a) the value of the individual's assets (at bank valuation)
    (b) the ability of the individual to meet the interest payments plus any capital repayment required.

20. The short run rate of interest is the three month inter bank rate. It is determined by the central bank's open market operations. The long run rate of interest is the yield on long dated gilt edged stocks.

21. It would supply cash at higher rates, in the main by supplying the market at the Treasury Bill tender and or by offering to repurchase Treasury Bills at lower market prices.

22. The effect on long run interest rates is not easily predictable. If an increase in short-term interest rates is seen as an attempt to reduce the future rate of inflation which is likely to the successful, then long run rates could fall or vice versa!

23. Rate of return is a combination of income and capital gain. Yield is a measure of income in relation to the price which has

to be paid to secure it, e.g. the dividend expressed as a percentage of current share price.

24. He means he wants to increase both the dividend and the share price.

25. A gilt-edged security has a fixed rate of interest but variable price. A treasury bill has no fixed rate of interest. Its yield is the difference between its current price and redemption value.

26. The rate of change in prices will be (d) 5%.

27. The rate of change in prices would be (b) 8%.

28. | Country | | Attractiveness |
|---|---|---|
| A | Russia | 6 |
| B | Bulgaria | 4 |
| C | Czechoslovakia | 2 |
| D | East Germany | 1 |
| E | Hungary | 3 |
| F | Poland | 5 |
| G | Romania | 7 |

Appendix A
Equilibrium: the difference between planned and actual

Equilibrium means unchanging. It is a key concept which under-pins thinking on the economy; it is crucial to the understanding of the dynamics in the system, in particular feedback loops.

First, some basic ideas from John Maynard Keynes (1936). If there is no international trade, then for any economy:

National income = consumption spending and investment spending
Investment spending = national income − consumption spending
But saving = national income − consumption spending
Therefore investment spending = saving

A nation's production is the same as its income. What is produced but not consumed, must be its investment; what is received in income but not spent on consumption is its saving. Therefore investment must be equal to saving.

It is a matter of logic that in a closed economy the amount actually invested must equal the amount actually saved. This is not necessarily equilibrium.

Think of humans – there is a great difference between what we plan and what we actually achieve.

Equilibrium is a situation where what we plan is what actually happens.

Disequilibrium is where one group in the system plans to do something different from another.

Because the economy is a set of linked markets, if households plan to save more than companies plan to invest, the whole level of economic activity (national income) will change until planned savings equals planned investment.

The process will work via the multiplier. If planned savings > planned investment, national income will fall until planned savings = planned investment (and actual savings = actual investment). If planned investment > planned savings, national income will rise until planned investment = planned savings.

This is a simple worked example, assuming a multiplier of 5. (This is based on a savings ratio of 20%).

national income	=	100
consumption	=	80
investment	=	20
savings	=	20

Start with equilibrium, i.e. planned and actual savings and investment are equal.

Now assume companies plan to invest only 15 (planned savings still 20).

We have disequilibrium and the economy changes to restore it.

Because companies plan to invest only 15, but households plan to save 20 (20% of total income) the level of national income will fall by 5 × the multiplier (=5) = £25

As national income falls, so does the income of households. They plan to save 20%. Equilibrium is restored when planned investment of 15 = planned savings = 20% of income (=20% of 75 = 15!)

In an open economy, national investment can exceed actual savings, where the difference is a capital inflow from abroad.

Country A is financing its investment using savings from Country B.

Under these circumstances the capital inflow will represent a surplus on the capital account of the balance of payments.

In the UK from 1986–89 domestic investment exceeded domestic savings; the consequence was an increased balance of payments deficit. For the world as a whole, actual savings must equal actual investment, but with an open system and free capital flows, it is not necessary for a country to achieve balance. Indeed, as a general rule countries with balance of payments deficits are investing more than they are saving and countries with balance of payments surpluses are saving more than they are investing. These flows have significant impact on relative exchange rates.

Appendix B
Is the economy a mechanical system or an organic system?

Scientists are discovering new ways of understanding how nature functions.

In particular they have discovered that natural systems are capable of endless variety because their dynamics are chaotic – unpredictable patterns emerge through a process of spontaneous self-organization, driven by dynamic feedback systems.

Natural scientists have discovered that simple feedback laws generate behaviour so complex that the links between cause and effect, action and outcome, simply disappear in the detail of unfolding behaviour. Nature, it would seem is continuously creative.

Economies are dynamic feedback systems driven by humans. The key question is whether feedback is positive or negative. Chaos is a fundamental property of non-linear feedback systems. Non-linear systems amplify positive feedback in some way, and the result is explosive, unstable equilibrium. However, negative or damping feedback is common in an economic system. For example, a company fixes a profits target and plans its business through its budgeting to achieve it. Through time, variances are calculated; and adverse variances prompt corrective action to bring the business back to its planned path. The budgetary system utilizes negative feedback to keep the organization on track. The same happens with the economy as a whole.

Remember the injection and withdrawals model:

WITHDRAWALS		INJECTIONS
Saving	>	Investment
Imports	=	Exports
Tax	<	Government Spending

Assume the balance of payments is in equilibrium. Now assume that the private sector decides to save more than it is currently investing, by £40 Bn in a full year.

With time-lags, retail sales growth will slow or go negative – there will be an unplanned stock build. Firms will begin to apply negative feedback by cutting their output; as they do so earnings will fall and the number of unemployed will increase. The Government sector takes the strain and damps the impact: tax revenues begin to fall (VAT receipts down) but Government spending begins to increase as unemployment payments rise. The Government runs a budget deficit which will (with no further discretionary action) equal £40 Bn. The system balances again, with a PSBR of £40 Bn financed from private sector savings.

When the private sector decides to raise its investment spending again, the reverse happens; the PSBR falls as the private sector deficit (savings < investment) increases. The system is using negative feedback to prevent disintegration.

However, if we change the assumptions, by allowing positive feedback via the exchange rate (i.e. an imbalance on the balance of payments) then the system is potentially explosive as self-reinforcing events take place in the foreign exchange and bond markets. It can be argued that, in 1987, Government put in negative feedback to prevent a collapse of the international economy after Black Monday (by increasing the supply of cash). And that the collapse of the ERM is an illustration of the system's behaviour when negative feedback is not applied in sufficient volumes. The biggest headache for all Governments is that the system changes through time. It is clearly an organic system because all human interactions take the form of feedback loops. The consequences of one action constitute non-linear feedback loops because people are emotional animals and always under or over-react. Since economies are simply a vast net of feedback loops between people, they must be capable of chaotic as well as stable and explosively unstable behaviour.

All economies are powerfully pulled in two fundamentally different directions.

To disintegration:

The principle of the division of labour suggests that economies can become more efficient and effective if companies divide tasks, segment markets, appeal to self-interest, motivate and empower people, and specialize by splitting into separate production units both in geographic and physical terms.

This process leads to fragmenting cultures, dispersed power and the Government finds it more and more difficult to apply effective negative feedback.

It can be argued that the fashion for deregulation, privatization, liberalization and power sharing at the local level is increasing economic instability.

To ossification:

To avoid the pull of disintegration and reap advantages of synergy and co-ordination, Government's 'Corporatism' pulls the state together and integrates the economic processes. National goals are stressed above individual, power is concentrated at the centre, communication and procedures are formalized and a strong shared national identity is established.

Such an economy becomes more and more rigid with over-regulation, rules, procedures, systems and control until it eventually ossifies.

Success lies somewhere between the two. It is best captured by the term 'mixed-market economy': the border between these two states. The political process in a democracy seems to produce swings between disintegration and ossification. Think of the UK: the corporatist seventies (ossification), the Thatcher self-interest years of the eighties (disintegration), the caring nineties (the balance?).

As the economy is driven by humans, then a learning process is always under way; learning and adaptation is a driver of negative and positive feedback, but it would appear that history repeats itself. Certainly boom and bust is the norm, based on two hundred years of economic development.

And yet for the period 1948–68 the global economy grew faster than ever before; Keynesian demand management techniques were being perfected to the extent that Governments could define full employment at 2.5% unemployed and deliver it by using fiscal and monetary policies to provide sufficient negative feedback.

These policies were said to have failed in the 1970s. The change in credit creation rules in 1971, followed by the quadrupling of the oil price in 1973 are examples of positive feedback loops which overwhelmed the negative (hence the argument that Government in the period was ineffective and their policies misplaced). One can argue that ossification was occurring by 1971 and the positive feedback pushed the system towards disintegration – with the popularity of Thatcherism the political outcome.

Looking at the Lawson boom years, it can be argued that the increase in interest rates in August 1988 took much longer to work than forecast, and as the behaviour of the UK banking system changed, a strong positive feedback loop came into play that was not widely understood and resulted in a deep recession not forecast by anyone.

The natural scientist would seek to explain our economic experiences by the use of chaos theory. Essentially, chaos means disorder and randomness in the behaviour of a system at a specific level, but a qualitative pattern at a general, overall level. The future unfolds unpredictably, but we recognize patterns. This is what we mean when we say history repeats itself. It does, but never in the same way. We recognize patterns of boom and recession, but each time they are different in specific terms, defying all attempts to predict them.

Chaos is the inseparable intertwining of order and disorder. Humans are able to cope because the order and disorder is bounded by recognizable patterns. Our memories do not store discrete shapes or events precisely; instead we store information about the strength of the connection between individual events perceived, which we combine to form concepts. We remember the irregular pattern, not the detail. This forms the basis of our actions, we view our world with experience-based intuition and the ability to detect analogies between one set of circumstances and another.

The world economy as a closed system

Figure B.1 (reproduced from Figure 8.3) shows the world as a closed system, but each component (economy) is interacting with the whole. There will be either positive or negative feedback as an economy, through its external flows, interacts with the whole

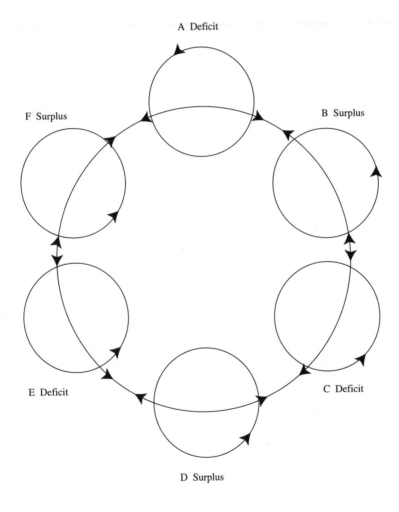

$$A+B+C+D+D+E+F=0$$

Figure B.1   The global system of payments

system. If we sum the external flows (measured in money terms) the result must be zero, by virtue of double-entry bookkeeping.

If country A is running a deficit on its current account, and its only trading partner is B, which is running a surplus, the two figures will be equivalent. Country A will need a surplus on its capital account and B a deficit on its capital account. The form this takes will always be different, but in a market system the deficit country would need to offer a higher return on capital than the surplus country to attract a currency inflow. The action to achieve this is, in itself, feedback either positive or negative.

An example in the 1990s is the massive inward investment into the UK from Japan, Germany and the USA. This allows the UK to run a (permanent) deficit on its current account. The investment flow is driven by higher prospective returns compared to that available in the donor country; the result of geography, political links (the UK's membership of the EC), low wages, relatively low employment cuts and attractive investment grants.

The inward investment flow is itself a feedback loop, whether positive or negative can be debated at length.

It can be agreed, however, that an open economy will produce more feedback than a closed economy and human experience to date suggests that free movement of capital is economically desirable.

But is the feedback it generates leading to global disintegration? The global economy is organic, its components have the capability to be continually creative. Global economic growth will continue as a consequence, but the relative positions of countries will be changing all the time, and there will be periodic shocks which will unleash feedback loops. It is impossible to state in advance whether the shocks will set up positive or negative feedback.

Appendix C
The problem of savings and investment behaviour

At this stage newcomers to economics often raise this question. Surely when individuals save, they expect a return, this can only happen if the savings are automatically invested?

Prior to 1932, it was the view of economists that savings were automatically invested. This view was certainly correct at the time it was formed (mid-1850s). Society was quite different 130 years ago. The owners of business saved from their current earnings (profits) to invest in the growth of the business. Their employees were usually not paid enough to save; there was saving to build houses – through the friendly society, but not the widespread saving we see today.

As society developed, the rising professional, managerial classes enjoyed increases in income, and with it, the ability to save. These groups were not owners of capital (most rented their houses) so their savings were placed with financial intermediaries such as banks and stock brokers.

This increasing complexity in society and income distribution caused a change in behaviour. Maynard Keynes in his general theory published in 1936 showed clearly that there was a significant economic effect where the amount some people planned to save would and could be different from the amount other people planned to invest. If these plans were misaligned and people planned to save more than companies planned to invest, a pool of idle savings would be the result and GDP, other things being equal, would fall. Keynes introduced a new way of thinking about the economy. Key to this is the concept of the multiplier which we covered in Appendix A.

Savings are not automatically invested. If there is excess saving the rate of interest should fall. (It depends on the Government's policy at the time, Governments can keep short-term interest rates up, despite excess saving).

A reduction in the rate of interest should reduce the level of saving. BUT this assumes the dominant reason for saving is the expected return. This is over simplistic.

What about fear, income in relation to age and number of dependants, habit and boosting the pension? All these factors influence an individual's planned savings.

And consider investment spending. Investment spending can be split into three categories:

1 Stocks of finished goods and raw materials
2 Capacity upgrading
3 Capacity expansion.

In terms of business financing, category 1 is a working capital decision, the other two are fixed asset decisions. The first can be planned or unplanned, the other two are always planned.

Consider planned investment in stocks of finished goods first. The general manager of a business may decide that sales will increase – he expects an economic upturn, he plans to raise his production, invest in stocks and then he will be poised to take advantage of increased customer demand just at the point it occurs. The result should be an increase in market share (if the competitors have read the market differently).

However, there are circumstances when the investment in stocks is unplanned. This is when demand falls from forecast levels and actual sales are below planned. The difference is an unplanned increase in stocks.

Investment in capacity upgrading is planned. It is often the result of Health and Safety or Environmental protection legislation or advances in technology which will result in greater efficiency (lowered unit cost). Companies always plan their investment.

Capacity creation is always planned. A view of future sales in relation to current capacity is formed. If it is expected that sales will be potentially greater than available capacity, then investment will take place.

How does the rate of interest influence investment spending?

An increase in the rate of interest will increase the cost of holding stocks if they are financed by bank overdraft. All other things being equal, one would expect existing stocks to be reduced if interest rates rise.

Investment in capacity upgrading if driven by legislation is not interest rate sensitive. The legislation will require compliance at or by a given date. Upgrading through the application of advanced technologies may be interest rate sensitive. But evidence suggests that the majority of upgrades are 'strategically essential' in order to keep up with the competition.

For capacity creation the rate of interest will be a factor, but is it a key driver?

We are, yet again, trying to understand behaviour. Based on the past, it would seem that the rate of interest has an influence but that there are considerable time-lags and all other things are not equal in the real world.

A rational (!) manager would conduct an investment appraisal. He may use a simple pay back method which calculates the number of years it takes for the cost of the investment (including interest) to be recovered. Or he may do a relatively more sophisticated discounted cash flow analysis.

This technique requires future cash flows associated with the investment to be guessed at. First, the useful life of the project has to be guessed; then for each year, the cash in less the cash out is calculated. For most projects, the net cash flow is negative in the earlier years, and strongly positive towards the end.

Assuming the residual value of the project is zero, the net cash in each year is discounted using a rate which is equal to the expected rate of interest, plus any premium for risk.

For example:

expected rate of interest	10%
discount rate	15%
(5% is the risk premium)	

Alternatively the discount rate is related to (or the same as) the return on capital employed a company requires. This is called the hurdle rate.

The discount rate is applied and the result is a present value of future net cash flows.

If the value is positive, the project is economically viable, if negative, non-viable.

The rational argument is that if expected interest rates are higher in the future, the discount factor has to be increased and net present value will be correspondingly lower or negative. Thus rising interest rates would reduce planned investment.

BUT, the whole exercise is based on expectations and a confident general manager would manipulate the figures to produce the desired result of his gut feeling that the project is a runner.

There are countless examples of this.

Think of petrol retailers; location of the filling station is the key to profitability. Really good sites are seldom available; when they are (with planning permission) it is strategically essential to own them. A company like Mobil or Total will quietly tell you that the normal investment appraisal rules tend to be reinterpreted; because the opportunity is too good to miss.

Because interest rates go up and down, it is always possible to choose an optimistic scenario if one really feels the investment should take place.

In 1987, 1988 and 1989 investment spending both absolutely and as a proportion of GDP rose substantially at a time of rising interest rates. Indeed, Nigel Lawson was surprised just how long it took the economy to cool down following rate increases.

Unfortunately this was the period when both the statistics for the recent past and the projection of the future started to go seriously off the rails.

The View from Number Eleven
Nigel Lawson

Investment at this time was interest rate insensitive because the majority were driven by an infectious optimism with expectations of increased return which was, for the majority, justified on the basis of projected incomes growth based on current rapid growth.

Appendix D
The Monetarist school and others

Theoretical economists divide into a number of camps on most economic issues. The relationship and causation between money and economic activity has been hotly disputed for at least two centuries and is still the subject of great debate amongst the Treasury Seven Wise Men who provide an economic think tank service to the Treasury economic policy makers.

The schools and what they believe
Pure Monetarist
The level of economic activity depends on the efficient operation of all markets. If markets work properly, the economy will always tend towards equilibrium (i.e. unchanged position) at the natural rate of unemployment. The natural rate of unemployment is the percentage of the labour force which it is necessary to have unemployed to act as a deterrent to those in employment to push for wage increases in excess of their productivity increases.

The Quantity Theory of Money defines the relationship between money and economic activity. It originally was expressed as an identity (which means one side of the coin is the same or equivalent to the other side or the amount spent equals the amount received). But subsequently (after some detailed econometric work by the Chicago School) it became an equation.

The identity:

$$MV \equiv PT$$

where   M is the amount of money
             V is the velocity of circulation
             P is the average price level

and   T is the number of transactions

All this says is that the amount of money multiplied by the number of times it gets spent is the same thing as the volume of transactions multiplied by their average selling price.

No economist would argue with this.

The equation:

$$M\bar{V} = \bar{P}T$$

The equation assumes that velocity is a constant. Then there is a direct relationship between M and PT (with a time-lag of up to a year).

The natural rate of unemployment suggests spare capacity. With spare capacity, P is a constant; in efficient markets prices will not rise if there is spare capacity.

Under these two assumptions there is a direct relationship between the volume of money and the volume of output until the level of unemployment falls below the natural level, at which point the price level will increase pro rata to the increase in money.

In simple terms, if the money supply is £50M, velocity is 3, then PT would be £150M.

If money stock increases to £100M, PT would be £300M, and if there was spare capacity, no inflation.

But if £300M = full employment of resources and money supply increases to £110M, then PT will be £330M, but the volume of transactions would be £300, and £30M would be absorbed by price increases. The inflation rate P, would be 10%.

The Cambridge approach

This was developed in the 1920s by Pigou and Marshall. They argued that the demand for money was a constant proportion of people's income and therefore that:

$V = \frac{1}{k}$. Thus if $K = \frac{1}{5}$, then $V = 5$, and a money supply of £100M would produce PT of £500M. If K were to change to $\frac{1}{3}$, then $V = 3$, and the result would be £300M.

The Cambridge approach recognizes in part the role of behaviour. It allows velocity to be determined by people's desire to hold money. But if K is constant, there is a direct relationship between the money supply and PT.

The Keynesians

John Maynard Keynes argued that V can be unstable as a result of people changing their liquidity preference. He wrote about this in 1936 in his *General Theory of Employment, Interest and Money*. It was in response to the apparent failure of monetary policy in the late twenties and early thirties to achieve growth in the economy.

Keynes argued that people demand money for a number of purposes.

1 **Transactions**. People demand money to finance living: to pay for their shopping, telephone, a few drinks, a meal out etc. As people receive their income in chunks (i.e. each month the salary is paid) but their expenditure is daily, there will always be a desire for money in its most liquid form.

The amount people will hold, Keynes argued, will depend on their income. As incomes rise, so will transactions' demand for money.

2 **Precautionary**. People hold money in liquid form just in case there is an unexpected bill – if, for example, the car needs a new gearbox or granny in Australia becomes ill.

Keynes argued that higher income groups will have a higher precautionary demand (i.e. a larger percentage of their income will be held in liquid form). This is because they run more expensive cars!

3 **Speculative**. Keynes introduced this concept to explain the lack of growth in the early thirties. It was a departure from the Cambridge School. Keynes suggested that people will hold money to speculate, i.e. they will hold money to purchase an asset if they consider the asset will then rise in price, thus giving them a capital gain.

Keynes used the gilt-edged market as the main example. If gilts are expected to rise in price, people use their money to purchase them. If gilts are expected to fall in price, they will sell (for cash, thus increasing their speculative demand).

The price of gilt-edged is inversely related to the rate of interest.

At low rates of interest (high gilt prices) people will hold money (speculative demand will be high). There is no point in buying gilts because their prices are expected to fall (the next movement in interest rates is expected to be upwards).

The speculative demand for money hypothesized by Keynes shows that at high rates of interest the demand for money is low.

Current thinking draws on all three schools of thought, as discussed in Chapter 10.

Appendix E
Stocks and flows

STOCKS AND FLOWS

At any point in time it is possible to measure the stock of money in the economy: for example, the Bank of England has a meter which measures the amount of notes and coin in issue. But the Bank cannot measure the flow of that money through the system. For anyone running a business it is always flow which matters. The flow is the dynamic of the system, driven by behaviour. In the case of money, velocity is all important. Nominal GDP is not determined by the stock of money alone. It is determined by the rate at which a unit of money (the stock) changes hands (the flow).

Similarly, it is possible to measure the stock of investment: the amount spent by companies on capacity. But it is the utilization rate of that investment which determines economic output. Utilization produces a flow of incomes.

Business forecasting is about guessing flows. Economic activity changes when flow changes.

SOME PROBLEMS WITH GDP AND STOCKS AND FLOWS

At the basic level, GDP = money × velocity adjusted for imports. Logic would suggest that £10 spent sixty times, would finance sales to the value of £600.

But GDP is not the value of total sales in the economy. It is the value of final sales. Thus sales of intermediate goods are not included in the final figure, GDP is the sum of added value, which is sales less cost of purchased raw materials, energy and services.

To measure the velocity of money, GDP at market prices is divided by the amount of money in issue. Using cash, the figure for the UK in 1993 is:

$$\frac{\text{GDP at market prices} \qquad 627\text{Bn}}{\text{Cash in circulation} \qquad 21.7\text{Bn}} = 28.8\times$$

Using broad money M4 (PLC money)

$$\frac{\text{GDP at market prices} \qquad 627\text{Bn}}{\text{Broad money} \qquad 549\text{Bn}} = 1.14\times$$

The GDP as measured is not the outcome of the number of times a unit of money changes hands. There are many transactions which we undertake which do not add value; for example, I sell my car for £3000; there is a transaction of £3000, but no added value.

However if I build a car from components purchased for £2000 and sell it for £3000, then there is added value of £1000 which would be the amount by which GDP increased.

In 1993 the sum of bank clearings, both automated (through BACS) and paper (cheques) was £26,613Bn; in the same year GDP was £627Bn. So the volume of transactions was 42.4× the value of final sales (GDP).

This is because a great many transactions add no value to the economic system. For example, if you purchase a share or bond from somebody it is a financial transaction but no value is added.

If the volume of transactions is £26,613Bn and broad money £549Bn, then its velocity is

$$\frac{25,613\text{Bn}}{549\text{Bn}} = 48.4\times$$

This indicates that a unit of money on average finances 48 transactions in a year. The stock of money generated flows 48 × its value.

One of the key questions on which economic analysis depends is to what extent do people make their borrowing and spending decisions on the basis of stocks and flows? Wealth is a stock, income is a flow.

Is it our wealth or our income or some combination of the two which drives our economic behaviour?

As yet there is no clearly defined answer to this question, but it is worth considering the issues. Much has been made of the 'feel good' factor by commentators in the early nineties. The lack of it is an explanation of why, despite economic recovery (an increase in flows) many players don't feel optimistic about the future. Based on discussions with a wide range of UK managers it would seem that the wealth effect is particularly important as a driver of the feel good factor.

70% of UK households are owner-occupier. The value of their house is their main source of wealth. If house prices rise faster than retail prices, the feel good factor is positive. Fears of loss of income (redundancy) are exaggerated at a time of static or falling house prices.

So a family's real income can be rising but not their feel good factor if their house is not increasing in price. This suggests that UK Governments should try and engineer an increase in house prices (by keeping interest rates low) whilst maintaining a stable RPI.

For households the stock of wealth (the value of fixed assets) is far greater in any given year than their flow of income. And in a deregulated financial services environment expenditure can exceed current income if capital assets are sold or borrowing takes place. If the feel good factor is strong, people will tend to spend more than their current income and finance it by borrowing, against the increase in the value of their capital assets.

Thus expenditure on goods and services is not solely determined by income and the flow of income can be increased if borrowing takes place or wealth is translated into income through asset sales.

Appendix F
Glossary of terms

Basis points 100 basis points = 1%. If interest rates are 10%, and they increase by 25 basis points, they become 10.25%.

Blue book the National Accounts published each year.

Deflation any measure taken by Government to reduce the rate of growth in spending in the domestic economy. Hence 'deflationary measures'. But strictly deflation is a prolonged fall in the general price level.

Deflationary gap the estimated difference between the ability of the economy to supply and current spending at a point in time. Supply exceeds demand.

Discretionary income income received by individuals after tax and after the standing charges of life e.g. mortgage interest, community taxes and utility changes. Sometimes called the leisure pound.

Discount houses a peculiar feature of the UK money market, not found in Frankfurt, New York or Tokyo. They began in the early 1800s, by accepting from merchants the right to a cargo due for delivery in two or three months time, for cash. Rapidly they became bill brokers – buying commercial paper at a discount for cash. They are today market makers who provide the banking system with cash on demand.

Discount houses get their cash by borrowing from large companies, banks, local authorities and the Bank of England. They use it to purchase short dated paper (treasury bills, short dated gilts, commercials bills and trade bills). They trade for immediate settlement, and therefore their holdings of paper is temporary.

In short, they are wholesalers of money who deal direct with the banking system and they are the only organizations in the City who have direct access to the Bank of England, i.e. are able to borrow on demand from the Bank. They make their profit on the difference between buying and selling prices of short dated paper (which determines the short-term interest rate). There are at least 425 Banks in London. The Bank of England finds it more convenient to move interest rates by dealing with the discount houses, knowing that very quickly the effect will spread throughout the market.

A discount house like Gerrard & National will at any time have on its book 'call money', 20–30 times its cash resources, so if there is a shortage of cash, it can quickly replenish it, by calling on the Bank of England.

Disposable income income received by individuals after tax.

Econometrics this is a branch of economic analysis which relies on the quantitative assessment of economic behaviour.

Equilibrium it means unchanging; and it is the starting point for most macro economic analysis: the economy is assumed at some point in time to be in equilibrium, then economists analyse the movement of the system to a different equilibrium.

Exogenous determined from outside the system. For example, if the price of oil rises sharply due to a war in the Middle East, this is an exogenous shock to the UK economy.

FT 100 or Footsie this is the top 100 companies in the FT 500 measured by market value.

FT 500 this is the Financial Times index of 500 quoted company shares. On any day the index can rise or fall.

Full funding this 'rule' was established in the early 1980s in the UK. It requires the Bank of England to sell gilt-edged securities equal to the value of net maturing debt, the PSBR and any underlying increase in foreign exchange reserves, to individuals and institutions outside the banks and building societies – otherwise known as the non-bank public.

G5 the Group of Five largest capitalist economies: USA, Japan, Germany, France and Britain.

G7 the Group of Seven : Group of Five plus Italy and Canada.

G10 the Group of Ten : Group of Seven plus Belgium, Holland, Sweden and an honorary 11th member – Switzerland.
Each group meets periodically to discuss international monetary arrangements and co-ordinate interest rate and exchange rate movements.

GDP Gross Domestic Product. This is an estimate of the value of final goods and services produced and sold in a country minus the value of imports. There is no allowance made for the depreciation of assets.

GNP Gross National Product. This is GDP plus net property income from abroad. It is a measure of all incomes flowing to residents of a country regardless of where the income is obtained.

Green book the UK Financial Statistics.

Hot money cash that is held in one currency but liable to switch to another at a moments notice.

IMF International Monetary Fund. Set up in 1944 at Bretton Woods. Consists of Finance Ministers of the major economies and aims to recycle funds from surplus countries to deficit countries to ensure free trade and stable exchange rates.

Inflationary gap the estimated difference between the ability of the economy to supply and current net spending on that supply, at constant prices and a given point in time. Demand exceeds supply.

Long-term interest rates this is determined by the yield on long dated gilt-edged securities.

Louvre Accord a meeting in Paris in 1987 held by G7 with the aim of stabilizing exchange rates relative to the dollar.

Minimum Reserve Requirement this is a control on German Bank lending. German banks are required to hold a minimum 12% of their liabilities in the form of reserve assets. It no longer applies in the UK.

Money stock an amount of money which exists in the system at a point in time. It can be in the form of cash (M0) or bank deposits (M4).

In 1993 in the UK,   M0 money stock was £22Bn
                                M4 money stock was £549Bn

MTFS Medium Term Financial Strategy.
    It was invented by Nigel Lawson in 1979 when he was first secretary to the Treasury. It was designed to put all Government income and spending decisions in the context of an overall financial plan with a ceiling on the PSPR. The aim was to reduce the rate of inflation over time by cutting the rate of growth in Government spending and raising income from privatization.

National debt the total amount of Government debt still outstanding. In the form of gilts, Granny Bonds, National Savings and Premium Bonds. Around 36% of GDP in 1992.

National Income the National Income is GDP plus net property income from abroad, minus taxes on expenditure plus subsidies, less a depreciation allowance.

Nominal nominal means in current prices. So nominal GDP is the value of final sales measured at current prices.

OECD Organisation for Economic Co-operation and Development. Membership is 24 of the most advanced countries. Based in Paris, it is a forum to discuss economic issues of mutual interest.

It produces authoritative economic forecasts twice a year on each member economy.

Petro-Dollars cash surpluses built up by oil exporting countries, following oil price increases in 1973 and 1979. These funds are liable to switch at a moments notice.

Pink book the balance of payments for the UK.

Plaza Accord in 1985 it met to agree that the dollar should be forced to weaken, through concerted intervention.

Printing money when the Bank of England sells gilt-edged or treasury bills to the banks and building societies they increase their assets but lose the cash equivalent, which the Government spends. However, the Bank of England will always purchase short dated gilts and treasury bills for cash from discount houses, which in turn purchase them from banks for cash. This process results in Government debt being 'monetized'. Underfunding means some of the debt is being monetized. The process results in the expansion of the money supply. The Full Funding rule prevents monetization. The Full Funding rule makes the impact of Government borrowing on the money supply neutral.

Privatization The Government offers for sale assets owned by the nation, to investors.

PSBR the Public Sector Borrowing Requirement.

It is the shortfall between Government expenditure and revenues. Financed by borrowing.

PSDR Public Sector Debt Repayment.

This is when Government revenue from tax exceeds Government spending. It allows some of the national debt to be repaid.

Red book the Financial Statement and Budget Report. Published at the time of the Budget in November. Contains useful background analysis by the Treasury.

Reflation any measure taken by Government to increase the level of spending in the domestic economy.

Repo rate this is the rate of interest which is established by the price the Bundesbank will pay to purchase commercial bills from banks. This is short for 'repurchase'. The Bank of England began to do the same in September 1992. It enables banks to borrow money direct from the Bank for two to five weeks. It is intended to extend this facility to all banks and building societies.

Round tripping this takes place when short-term rates are lower than long term. Corporate Treasurers borrow short-term money and buy long dated gilts.

Short-term interest rates these rates are determined in the wholesale money market by the activities of the Bank of England. The bench mark is the 3 month inter bank rate.

Sterilization this means sell gilt-edged securities equal to the value of intervention on the foreign exchange market. If the Bank of England buys 1 million D-Marks in exchange for sterling, at a rate of say 2Dm=£1, then it would need to sell gilt-edged to the value of £$\frac{1}{2}$million to 'mop-up' the additional pounds.

Treasury bill for over 100 years the UK Government has used TBs to raise money and regulate the liquidity of the banking system. A tender is held weekly, but bills are also issued each working day by the Bank of England on behalf of the Treasury.

A TB is secure, liquid and yields a return. It is also a bearer document which means it is convenient, because it can change hands for cash on delivery. Because of these advantages, the rate of interest is lower than for a gilt-edged. A purchaser of TBs, unless a discount house, cannot encash his TB before the due date. A discount house will accept TBs for cash immediately (and the discount house can get a TB cashed before its maturity date at the Bank of England).

A TB is issued for 91 days, in denomination ranging from £5000–£1000,000. There is no fixed rate of interest. The rate of interest is the difference between the purchase price and the redemption value.

Under funding This means financing part of the PSBR, plus maturing debt plus the increase in reserves by selling gilt-edged to the banks and building societies.

Unsterilized intervention the Bank of England sells pounds for D-Marks and leaves the pounds in the market.

Velocity of money this is a simple ratio which indicates on average the amount of GDP a unit of money finances over a period of time.

It is usually $\dfrac{\text{Nominal GDP}}{\text{Money Stock}}$

so if nominal GDP is £600Bn and the money stock is £500Bn the velocity is

$$\frac{600\text{Bn}}{500\text{Bn}} = 1.2 \text{ times}$$

World Bank alternative name for the International Bank for Reconstruction and Development. Set up in 1944 at Bretton Woods, to assist in post-war reconstruction. Now funds selective projects in newly industrializing countries.

Further reading

Hutton, W. (1995) *The State We're In*, Jonathan Cape.
Lawson, N. (1992) *The View from No 11*, Bantam Press.
Morris, M. (ed) (1983) *The UK Economic System*, 3rd edn, OUP.
Omerod, P. (1994) *The Death of Economics*, Faber & Faber.
Stewart, M. (1986) *Keynes and After*, 3rd edn, Penguin.